COMPUTERS
AND
EDUCATION

By
James L. Poirot

STERLING
SWIFT publishing company
1600 fortview road
austin, texas 78704

©1980

STERLING
SWIFT publishing company

ISBN#0-88408-137-0

TABLE OF CONTENTS

PREFACE   iii

I. HISTORICAL OVERVIEW   1
   Introduction   1
   Funding   3
   Types of Computer Facilities   4
   Regional Service Centers   6

II. COMPUTER APPLICATIONS FOR INSTRUCTION   7
   Introduction   7
   Computer Assisted Instruction   8
   Types of CAI   10
   CAI Authoring Packages   11
   Advantages and Problems of CAI   12
   Computer Instruction for the Student   14

III. COMPUTER LITERACY   17
   Introduction   17
   Computing Competencies Needed by Teachers   17
   Computing Competencies Needed by Students   19
   Program Goals in Computer Education   22

IV. SOFTWARE AVAILABILITY   25
   Introduction   25
   Selection of Software   27
   Quality Software Guidelines   27

V. COMPUTER APPLICATIONS FOR EDUCATIONAL ADMINISTRATION   31
   Introduction   31
   Student Master File   32
   Class Attendance   34
   Grading and Grade Analysis   35
   Grade Reporting   38
   Scheduling   38
   Payroll   39
   Non-Payroll Services   42
   Administrative Recommendations   44

VI. EDUCATIONAL GAMES   47
    Introduction   47
    Movin' On   47
    Computer Bingo   49
    I Have – Who Has   51
    Bugs   54
    Hands-Up   56
    Hexapawn   59
    Cardiac   64

VII. CURRENT TRENDS   69
    Introduction   69
    Integrated System Design   70
    Microcomputer Laboratory   72
    Computer Laboratory Centers   78
    Role of the Laboratory Teacher   79
    Selecting a Microcomputer   80
    Supplemental Laboratory Activities   81

BIBLIOGRAPHY   85

INDEX   88

PREFACE

The computer is now well established in most school systems across the country. Instructional computer applications, computer literacy and computer use in school administrative functions have all attributed to the rapid expansion of computer technology within education. The development of the inexpensive microcomputer system has placed the cost of the computer within reach of every school. With the expense of computers no longer being an overriding and limiting factor, we see another major problem to be addressed in computing education-- teacher computer literacy. The vast majority of our teachers received their education prior to the microcomputer "revolution" and hence have had little or no formal training in computing. This text is designed to aid teachers and administrators in becoming familiar with the use of the computer in education.

Educational applications in instruction and administration are included. "Computer Assisted Instruction" and "Computer Literacy" are discussed and computer related games are introduced. All topics are covered at a "Computer Introductory" level so that no prior computing experience is required. This text should be helpful to the individual using it for self study, within a college level course or within an inservice training program for teachers.

The author would like to extend his appreciation to many colleagues and students who helped in the drawing together of materials for this work. Particular thanks go to David Groves, Carin Horn, Don Retzlaff, Ann Easterling, D'Anna Shaver, Janet Holt, Nell Berry, Sunnye Murdock and Charyla Dickey. The

Hurst-Euless-Bedford Independent School District, sponsored by a grant from the Sid Richardson Foundation, provided support for research into some of the areas studied. Dr. Forest Watson and Mr. Ronnie Banner of H-E-B deserve special thanks. Most importantly, I thank my wife, Peggy, and my family for their continuing support.

I
HISTORICAL OVERVIEW

INTRODUCTION

The Mark I, developed at Harvard University, was the first electromechanical digital computer and became fully operational in 1945. Several years later, in 1950, there were only 12 computers in the United States. By 1960, the number had risen to 6,000. Today there are more than 75,000 large general purpose computers and hundreds of thousands of microcomputers in use throughout the United States.

Not only have the numbers of computers increased, but there have also been dynamic advances in the complexity of the technology itself. Today's computers are hundreds of thousands of times faster, more reliable, and more cost efficient than the Mark I. (The Central Processing Unit of the Mark I cost $750,000 in 1944.)

Uses of computer technology in an information society are pervasive. They are used throughout the sciences, business, industry, government, transportation, law, medicine, and education. By 1978, more than 30 percent of all secondary schools utilized the computers for instruction, and computer literacy was being advocated as the fourth "basic skill" of the impending 21st Century.

The first educational application of the com-

1

puter came in the area of school administrative functions. Such functions as payroll, tax accounting and attendance are essentially "business" related. With public business and industry utilizing computers cost effectively, it was only natural that this efficiency be taken advantage of in education.

In the late 50s and early 60s, Computer Assisted Instruction (CAI) was introduced at selected sites across the country--generally at the university level. In the mid-60s, attempts were made to move CAI down to the pre-college students to increase the children's skill levels. However, CAI was still considered to be largely experimental. Cost of the computer equipment simply inhibited widespread utilization. The microcomputer system introduced in the 1970s has now placed the cost of CAI at a level where all school districts can afford its use. CAI is no longer a luxury of only a few but is now considered by many as a necessary supplemental source for quality education.

The computer revolution has provided job opportunities for hundreds of thousands. These employment opportunities and the need to learn about this new technology have caused school districts across the country to implement computer related curriculum. In the late 60s, courses entitled Computer Mathematics, Computer Data Processing, etc., were found in many of the country's schools. In the 80s Computer Literacy is a course which will likely be found at most schools and at several grade levels.

Computer technology reaches further and influences more than just CAI and computer instruction. During the past several years, new and improved methods of information delivery have helped to bring educational instruction to a great many individuals. Communication satellites have been used to transmit curricula and special programs to large urban areas and to such remote sites as Alaska, the Pacific Islands, and the Appalachians. Such systems have also been used for satellite conferences and meetings between educational groups, government representatives, and student bodies. Telecommunications computer networks have facilitated the sharing of resources, course work, and scientific/educational research at all levels of education.

In a similar manner, "electronic blackboards" have linked instructors and off-site students without the need for costly travel. The development of videotapes and videodiscs and their computer interfacing may result in one-time investments for equipment capable of serving as high volume, interactive information storage and retrieval sources of educational materials. Television, via broadcast or cable, continues to be a familiar medium for providing inexpensive mass dissemination of educational programs and learning experiences. The capabilities of interactive, computer-based television systems for educational purposes are being tested and put into operation in certain locales.

Technology in the classroom (and resistance to change) is not a new concept in the educational process. Books, blackboards, charts, maps, filmstrips, motion pictures, phonographs, tape recorders, and language laboratories can all be classified as instructional tools; and, for the most part, each is now widely accepted as an aid to teaching. Newer forms of educational technology, and more specifically computers, have not yet fared as well in their acceptance. Some of the negative reactions may be due in part to the previous failure of such technologies to achieve their full potentials in educational areas during the 1950s and 1960s. The previous difficulties of integrating man-machine techniques into established teaching methods and the normal psychological resistance to change, coupled with expensive costs for implementation, have delayed wide-scale computer applications in education.

FUNDING

Early support for computers came from the National Science Foundation (NSF), which in 1954 began to support computerized science education. The United States Office of Education also began funding research and demonstration projects in education that same year. By the 1960s, many university campuses had received federal assistance, and by 1962, 200 colleges had established computer centers.

Many sources have invested in the research and development of computers in education. The following figures are an indication:

- The United States Office of Education alone spent an estimated $161 million between 1964 and 1969 for the use of computers in education.
- In the same years, an estimated $685 million was spent by the United States Office of Education on educational technology and related projects.
- The National Science Foundation has specifically supported the development of computer-related innovational projects in education with nearly $40 million since 1965.
- In institutions of higher learning, an estimated $480 million was spent for computing activities since 1965.
- A conservative estimate of overall national investment in educational uses of computers may be approximately $2 billion.

TYPES OF COMPUTER FACILITIES

To some extent, the type of computer facilities available in a school will determine the type of instructional uses to which the computer may be put. It is first necessary to understand the three general types of facilities: "batch," "on-line," and "microcomputers."

Batch systems usually consist of a relatively large computer system with a card reader for input and a line printer for output. Programs are submitted to an operator who runs the programs through the computer at a convenient time. The results are returned to the user at some later time. Often there is a delay ranging from a few minutes to several days. The facilities may be located several miles away from the school or may be relatively close by.

Obviously, the user cannot personally interact with the computer. If there are errors in the results or changes the user wants to make, then he/she must wait and resubmit the program. The two main disadvantages of the batch system are the inability

4

of the students to interact with the computer directly and the rather long time between the submission of the program and receiving the computer output.

A key consideration in batch systems is the turn-around time. That is, how long does it take to get a program run? If it is a few minutes or less (which is standard at some universities) the system is much more suited to instructional use than if the turn-around time is "overnight" or several days. A major problem with teaching computer programming on a batch system is that of keeping the students involved in constructive learning activities while they are waiting for the return of their programs. A "feedback" delay of several hours or days is discouraging to most students. Another problem might be the language available on the system. The most common programming languages available for batch systems and suitable for students are FORTRAN and COBOL. BASIC, which is currently the most popular language for teaching students at the secondary level, is usually not available. (Note that this need not be the case. Batch processing BASIC systems do exist on some computers.)

Batch systems are not suitable for running computer assisted instruction (CAI) packages because of the need for immediate interaction. However, batch systems are quite suited to the running of most packaged programs. Most batch computer systems have extensive libraries of packaged programs.

"On-line" or interactive computer facilities consist of a computer and some sort of terminal (connected to the computer) such as a cathode ray tube (CRT). The computer system may be a one terminal minicomputer or a time-shared system. A terminal usually serves as both input and output device. It must be located in an area where students can have access to it (such as a classroom). However, the computer may be several miles or even hundreds of miles away, connected to the terminal by way of a telephone hook-up. This set-up functions as if the computer were in the same location with the users.

If the facilities are "on-line" then all three of the instructional uses (programming, CAI, and packaged programs) can be implemented to some ex-

5

tent. Program construction requires very little in
the way of size and can be implemented as long as a
suitable language is available. Packaged programs
can be used with minimum facilities also. There may
be a few packaged programs which are too large for a
very small computer, but there are still a large
number which can be used.

The microprocessor chip was first developed in
1971, but it was not until 1977 that a complete off-
the-shelf microcomputer system was available for
educational use. Since 1977, however, we have truly
seen a microcomputer revolution in education. Thousands of Apples, TRS-80s, PETs, TI99/4s, and others
have been purchased by school districts across the
country. Most systems are being utilized for Computer Assisted Instruction and/or computer programming. Even though existing educational software for
microcomputers is now a problem, this problem will
be alleviated as more educators obtain hardware to
perform their own software development.

REGIONAL SERVICE CENTERS

Due to the extreme cost of large computer systems, individual schools can normally not afford the
luxury of owning their own large system. As a result, some school regions have used the approach of
sharing the cost and utilization of a large computer
facility through a Regional Service Center. Such
centers are organized to provide the opportunity to
school districts within that region to participate
in specialized services that would otherwise be beyond the reach of their average school system.

Centers can help organize and manage class
scheduling, grade reporting, test scoring, employee
payroll, attendance accounting, finance, tax accounting, inventory accounting, classroom test scoring,
public opinion polling, information retrieval, and
vocational education. Computer Assisted Instruction
is also generally available and student instructional terminals enable students to take a number of
courses "on-line."

II
COMPUTER APPLICATIONS FOR INSTRUCTION

INTRODUCTION

Computer use in education was foreseen years ago; it arrives at last because computers have been improved, made smaller, and produced considerably cheaper over the last five years. Yet, many of the questions raised in the minds of those who foresaw what was coming remain unanswered. How will use of computers affect the child's development? What are appropriate languages for young children to use in talking with computers? What devices other than the traditional keyboard and screen or terminal/printer can, when attached to a computer, maximize its educational utility for the young child? What should teachers know about computers? How expert should a teacher be in computing to make reasonably effective use of it in teaching and learning? What is the teacher's role in a classroom where every student has free access to computing facilities? What is the impact of computer games on the child and what role should games have in school? When should the computer be used as a tool, when as a tutor, and when as a tutee?

Within a few years every child in America is likely to have at least one personal computer. The potential impact upon schools staggers the imagination. At the least, it is likely to move the focus

7

of education from the end product to process and
raise visual and auditory forms of information to a
status rivalling that of written language. Because
ideas can be presented, explored, and expanded by
human interaction with the computer, computing is
certain to transform the schools from kindergarten
upwards.

Since the arrival of the first electronic digital computer in 1945, educational researchers have
studied its applications as an educational tool.
Although some teachers are apprehensive lest they be
completely replaced in our schools by impersonal
computer terminals, even the severest critics of the
present status of educational technology admit that
the computer will eventually have a large impact on
education. Most computer educators believe that
there are important roles for the teacher which cannot be usurped by a machine: strengthening between
student relationships, changing perceptions towards
those about us, evaluating and encouraging artistic
expressions; therefore, education must revolve
around the teacher who will increasingly make use of
the computer as a powerful teaching tool.

Figure 2.1   Personal Computer System

An educational tool is valuable only if it can help the teacher to do a better job than can be done without it. Films, television and slides are valuable because as educational tools they can help bring into the classroom experiences which the teachers cannot. The teacher weighs the availability, convenience, cost and effectiveness of these tools in deciding whether or not to make use of them for a particular lesson. What is it, then, that the computer can do that warrants its use as a classroom tool?

COMPUTER-ASSISTED INSTRUCTION

Computer-assisted instruction, known most commonly by the letters CAI, refers to the use of computers in teaching. It does not involve teaching about computers, but rather, using computers as an aid in the classroom instruction of a particular subject matter.

Figure 2.2   CAI Laboratory

Dartmouth, Stanford, and Florida State University were early leaders in the field of CAI with their work beginning in the late 50s and early 60s. Florida State used a newly developed high-level CAI language called Coursewriter to implement complete university level courses in physics and statistics. At the same time, Dartmouth developed the BASIC language, a simplified programming language that could be easily learned. This language aided in the development and usage of CAI because of its simplistic nature. In the mid-60s, Stanford took a new approach by applying CAI in a different area. Rather than working with university students, they worked with pre-college students in an effort to increase the children's skill levels in English and math.

In the 70s, interest in CAI continued to spread throughout the United States, and even more progress is expected in the 80s. The Minnesota Educational Computer Consortium at Lauderdale, Minnesota, is involved in a continuing program for both college and pre-college students. Among its most useful projects is an extensive study comparing the cost, capabilities, and educational uses of microcomputers. This study, and others like it, has shown that the development of the microcomputer may be the technological breakthrough which will allow CAI to be accessible to most classrooms in the near future.

California State University at Fresno is involved in acquiring, modifying, and sharing quality CAI materials in a wide range of fields on the secondary and college levels. Many of their programs have been distributed to schools across the United States. Also producing a significant amount of software has been the University of California at Irvine, under the direction of Alfred Bork.

One of the most established CAI projects in the world is the PLATO system, which is funded by the National Science Foundation. Three major PLATO installations are located at the University of Illinois, Florida State University at Tallahassee, and the University of Delaware, with other smaller installations scattered about the country. PLATO uses the high level language, TUTOR, which enables programmers to produce complex CAI material including such features as animation and voice output.

TYPES OF CAI

There are three major types of CAI systems: drill and practice, simulation, and tutorial. Often a teacher presents a concept to students which can best be understood and retained by repetitive practice. In this situation, a CAI drill and practice program is most helpful. When using a drill and practice, it is assumed that the material covered in the program has been previously discussed in the classroom. This type of CAI material is more easily acquired from outside sources than the other types, because it is the easiest form to write.

Simulation programs are especially helpful in scientific experiments. Instead of using a lab for conducting these projects, the experiments can be performed in a simulated form using computers. Results of the experiment are displayed on the terminal screen. Simulation adds new dimensions to experiments and to their use in teaching, because it makes visible many very small, very slow, or very rapid changes which cannot be observed in actuality. The time scale of events can be expanded or contracted thousands of times. Simulation programs are not limited to science, but may be included in teaching sociology, medicine, statistics, business, mathematics, journalism, and others.

CAI tutorial systems present material to the student, and then ask him/her to answer questions concerning the information. It is not assumed that a student has prior knowledge of a subject. In some exercises, printed material is provided along with the computer program so that the student has something to study when away from the terminal. If a student correctly answers questions over the material, he/she may progress through the program at a rapid rate. If a correct answer is not given, he/she is branched to another part of the program which will give additional help on the material. Tutorial systems may be used either independently of, or in conjunction with, the classroom teacher. They provide an excellent approach in helping students with make-up work.

Two additional terms often heard when discussing types of CAI are adjunct and primary. Adjunct CAI supplements the learning process by supporting or illustrating concepts. One example of adjunct CAI might be a drill and practice program which is short in duration and supported by instruction in a regular classroom. Primary CAI can be independent of classroom instruction and is usually longer in duration. This type is generally less well known in the education field, but it is sometimes seen, especially on the college level, in courses which are completely taught by computer.

CAI AUTHORING PACKAGES

The designer or author of a CAI lesson does not have to be a computer programmer. Although programming languages such as BASIC may be used for CAI development, most computer systems have available an "authoring" software package. Such a package is designed so that teachers with little or no programming experience can develop CAI courseware. PILOT, Coursewriter, IDF and TUTOR are some example package names.

Various CAI authoring packages differ in some respects. However, all are designed for easy use. The teacher or author is generally "prompted" by the package to provide textual material, questions, answers, responses to correct answers, wrong answers, responses to wrong answers, hints, etc. The primary function of the author is to design good interactive instructional material while the package does the "programming" part.

After the CAI lesson has been developed, the package then administers the lesson to the student. Statistics such as the number of correct answers, the number of hints given, etc., may be retained by the package and later provided to the teacher.

ADVANTAGES AND PROBLEMS OF CAI

There are several advantages of computer teaching over the conventional classroom. Classroom teaching must be instructor-centered so that students have to proceed at the speed and level of complexity of the instructor. Brighter students find the pace too slow and are bored, while those not-so-bright often become lost or fail to understand part of what is said. Any student can miss sections through lapses in attention. But with computer assisted education, the process is pupil-centered, and the machine adapts its pace to that of the student. The slow student can ask for endless repetition without embarrassment, and the machine will retrace its steps with infinite patience. On the other hand, the quick student can skip a segment with the machine questioning to check that he/she does, in fact, know it. With a well-produced CAI program, the student is unlikely to become bored or distracted. The machine will be programmed to ask frequent questions and grade the difficulty of its demands according to the ability displayed. If a long time is taken for a reply to a question, the program can send prodding messages. The student cannot race ahead without a true understanding of the material because the program constantly examines the level of understanding.

The computer can also free the teacher from certain tedious chores, allowing more time to spend in personal interaction with students. Even though most students are attracted to the computer because it is a refreshing change of pace from normal modes of instruction, this human contact offered by the teacher is still the most important element in stimulating creative abilities.

There are major problem areas related to the application of computers in education: (1) facilitating man-machine communication, (2) cost efficiency, and (3) user acceptance.

Two factors make it difficult for people to communicate with machines. First, the terminals are not appropriate for some educational applications and, second, the language that a computer understands is not appropriate to the user. The most popular input/output device is the terminal or CRT. The cathode-ray tube tends to have poor resolution and may be difficult for young children to read for extended periods. The best might be the non-impact printer which makes use of electrostatically charged ink sprayed on paper because it is fast, quiet, and easy to read; but it is still too expensive. Fairly good sound quality is available in computer-manipulated vocal sounds; the technique is used in such applications as telephone number references and in bank account or charge account verification systems.

Computer programmers become quite skilled at computer languages, but are often not qualified to write effective CAI programs. Languages that are easier to use have had to be developed for teachers who wish to write CAI programs, but who know little about computers or programming. Professional educators, not programmers, will have to raise the standard and improve the style of computer assisted instruction.

The benefits of CAI must be greater than the costs if investment in such systems will be considered feasible. Here the choice of the type of computers used is important. Large computer systems generally cost much more than microcomputer systems, but will also have more courseware available. The type of terminal--color or black and white--will not only affect cost but effectiveness of delivery of the courseware. Graphics capability on a CAI system should be examined closely, for such capability will affect the quality and cost of the CAI. As technology advances, the cost of terminals will surely come down. Observing the cost trend of hand calculators is encouraging with hopes that terminals will follow that trend. Communications cost is another element, particularly when the CAI system is on a time-sharing basis. This cost does not seem likely to go down very quickly, although work on communication satellites and laser communications may someday alleviate this problem. Probably the most expensive cost element is the development, maintenance, and upkeep of high quality written materials and computer software. For example, it has been estimated that an average of two hundred hours of author time is involved in the development of one hour of student console time. There does not appear to be any easy solution to this problem.

Some people are not willing to accept the computer as an aid for instruction. They may claim that extensive use of computer technology may lead to impersonalized teaching. This could happen, but it is very likely that it will make learning and teaching more personalized because computer systems will be able to offer highly individualized instruction. Another common claim is that widespread use of computers will lead to excessive standardization of education. Again this is a possibility, but it can provide a means of raising educational standards in schools. More importantly, the wide use of computers can introduce a wide variety of educational and intellectual experiences. Finally another opposition is that CAI will bring us closer to becoming slaves of machines. However, computers can free students from the drudgery of doing exactly similar tasks that do not fit their individual needs.

It should be emphasized that while some subjects lend themselves well to computerized teaching, others may not. Computer assisted instruction will never replace the human teacher. It is up to educators to recognize both the usefulness and limitations of computers in education.

COMPUTER INSTRUCTION FOR THE STUDENT

Computer Assisted Instruction is primarily concerned with the "Teaching With Computers"; there is also another area of instructional computing that we may title "Teaching About Computers." There are currently four instructional areas where such teaching occurs--Computer Mathematics, Computer Data Processing, Vocational Data Processing and Computer Literacy.

Computer Mathematics is currently the most commonly found course on computer instruction at the secondary school level. Even though the course is taught by mathematics teachers and is a mathematics course elective, it most often resembles an "Introduction to Computer Programming" course.

Topics vary from computer history, flowcharting and programming to machine logic design. BASIC is the computer language most often being used and with the microcomputer influence, it will likely continue to be the most popular.

Computer Data Processing is a course taught within the business curriculum while Vocational Data Processing is found in some vocational related programs. The data processing areas emphasize business applications, COBOL as a language, and computer systems operations.

While the above three courses are generally concentrated at the secondary school level, Computer Literacy is a topic taught throughout the K-12 grade levels. It is felt that Computer Literacy will be the primary topic of instruction in computing education of the future. Thus we include an entire section on this topic.

III
COMPUTER LITERACY

INTRODUCTION

Computer literacy is a new area of knowledge that includes (1) an understanding of the technology used when processing information, (2) an understanding of the effects that computers have had and will have on society, and (3) an understanding of how computers are problem-solving tools. Computer literacy is becoming a process of making intelligent, productive, and creative decisions about computer technology. The degrees to which individuals are "computer literate" vary greatly according to their competencies.

COMPUTING COMPETENCIES NEEDED BY TEACHERS

On December 4-5, 1978, the Elementary and Secondary Schools Subcommittee (ES[3]) of the Association for Computing Machinery (ACM) Curriculum Committee met in Washington, D.C., to begin the process of formally laying out. curricular and teacher training guidelines for the integration of computing into American elementary and secondary schools. Teacher competencies to be achieved in computing were defined, qualified, and differentiated for specific

instructional groups. The following comments are a
summary of the ES^3 Report on "Computing Competencies
for School Teachers," February 1980.

The competencies which are universal in scope
and which are seen to be needed by all teachers and
educational administrators regardless of discipline
represent immediate goals for education. These are
the computing competencies which all school teachers
should have to teach effectively in a society perme-
ated by computers:

• Be able to read and write simple programs that work
  correctly and to understand how programs and sub-
  programs fit together into systems;
• Have experience using educational application software and documentation;
• Have a working knowledge of computer terminology,
  particularly as it relates to hardware;
• Know by example, particularly in using computers in
  education, some types of problems that are and some
  general types of problems that are not currently
  amenable to computer solution;
• Be able to identify and use alternate sources of
  current information on computing as it relates to
  education;
• Be able to discuss at the level of an intelligent
  layperson some of the history of computing, particularly as it relates to education; and
• Be able to discuss moral or human-impact issues of
  computing as they relate to societal use of computers generally, and educational use particularly.

Competency levels for those instructors who are
teaching computing as a subject are similar to those
of a computer professional. In addition to teaching, however, these individuals are also a general
resource for computer-related information for faculty, administration, and students. The core concepts
listed below are in addition to an enhanced version
of general teacher competency levels:

• Be able to write and document readable, well struc-
  tured individual programs and linked systems of two
  or more programs;
• Be able to determine whether they have written a
  reasonably efficient and well organized program;
• Understand basic computer architecture;
• Understand the range of computing topics that are

18

suitable to be taught as well as the justification
for teaching these topics;
•Know what educational tools can be uniquely employed in computer science education;
•Develop the ability to assist in the selection,
acquisitions and use of computers, interactive
terminals and computer services which are suitable
to the enhancement of instruction; and
•Be able to assist teachers in evaluation, selection, and/or development of appropriate instructional materials which utilize computing facilities.

The level or subject competencies specific to
each discipline include an extensive array of possibilities. A general awareness of computers in educational research, administration, and instruction
(drill-and-practice, games, tutorials, and simulations) will assist in developing useful competencies. In terms of these subject-specific competencies, the teacher should:
•Be able to use and evaluate the general capabilities of the computer as a tool for pursuing various
discipline- or level-specific educational tasks;
•Be able to use and evaluate alternative hardware
and software systems designed to function as tutors
or teacher aids;
•Be familiar with alternative hardware and software
systems designed to perform school administration;
and
•Be familiar with information and quantitative techniques of study in the (teachers') subject.

COMPUTING COMPETENCIES NEEDED BY STUDENTS

To date the majority of computer-related subjects like computer mathematics, computer data processing, vocational data processing, and computer
literacy are taught by mathematics teachers. The
National Council of Teachers of Mathematics has recently published its formal recommendations for
school mathematics for the 1980s. Herein, it is
suggested that:
•Mathematics programs must take full advantage of

the power of calculators and computers at all grade
levels;
• Beyond an acquaintance with the role of computers
and calculators in society, most students must obtain a working knowledge of how to use them, including the ways in which one communicates with
each and commands their services in problem-solving;
• With the increasing availability of microcomputers
at decreasing costs, it is imperative that schools
play an active part in preparing students of the
1980s to live in a world in which more and more
functions are being performed by computers; and
• A computer literacy course, familiarizing the students with the role and impact of the computer
should be a part of the general education of every
student.

Computer literacy will soon be taught as a subject throughout the educational system. The approach
and content of these courses and instructional units
will vary widely. It is generally agreed that the
subject include an understanding of the capabilities,
limitations, applications, and implications of computers. It is strongly suggested that "hands-on"
experiences be provided for the learners and that
the computer be presented as a problem-solving tool.
The following major topics should be included in any
computer literacy course:

Computer History. A computer literacy course
should include historical highpoints of computer development. In general, knowledge of computer facts
should be studied along with the time line of other
technological advancements and special occasions.

Computer Systems. At the completion of a computer literacy course, a student should know the
major components of a computer system. In addition,
the student should be able to explain the function
of each component and give examples of each component. The student should also come away with a basic
understanding of what happens to a program as it
proceeds through the components that make up the
computer system. The student should be able to dif-
ferentiate between hardware and software and should
also be aware of the types of software available.

Problem Solving. During the computer literacy
course the student should be exposed to the five-

step approach to problem solving. The student should also be expected to apply this approach to programming problems. This five-step approach requires that the student be able to understand the problem, to plan a strategy for solving the problem, to code that strategy into some language, to test the program, and to prepare the program and possible solution for use by others (documentation).

Limitations of the Computer. Every student that has completed a computer literacy course should become aware that the computer is only as good as the programs that go into it. In effect, the student should be aware that the computer is a tool to be used by a human in the solving of a problem. The computer is not the solution.

Applications in Society. No computer literacy course would be complete without addressing this topic. Each student should be made aware that there is hardly any occupation that is not affected by a computer. Students should explore computer usage in many areas including: education, research, weather prediction, creative arts, government, medicine, business, libraries, law enforcement, military defense, transportation, engineering, and recreation. The student should also be encouraged to investigate the types of functions a computer can perform in the above mentioned fields, and also encouraged to speculate as to other computer possibilities.

The student should also investigate the effect computers have on personal life, now, and what effect they may have in the future. The student should be encouraged to study (and perhaps criticize) the computer as a tool for amassing large amounts of personal information about individuals. The effect the computer will have upon future career choices is another topic not to be overlooked.

Possible Threats. In studying the applications of the computer in society the student should also be presented with the concept of computer crime. What types of computer crime exist now? What effect does it have on the individual? How can it occur? What can be done to control it? Other possible threatening circumstances should be presented to the computer literacy student. Will the computer affect our national employment figures? Is a large personal

information bank good?　Are there any privacy rights
for the individual?

PROGRAM GOALS IN COMPUTER EDUCATION

The following goals in computer education were
developed by the Tri-County Goal Development Project—Portland, Oregon.　They are included here for
reference and discussion.
(1) The student knows events that have influenced or
    may influence computer development and use.
(2) The student relates knowledge about computers to
    career goals and plans.
(3) The student knows characteristics of computer-
    related hardware, software, and documentation,
    and principles underlying their design and use.
(4) The student knows theoretical aspects of com-
    puter science appropriate to the student's level
    of computer use.
(5) The student knows applications and uses of com-
    puters.
(6) The student knows effects of computers on soci-
    ety.
(7) The student knows principles, procedures, and
    limitations of computer systems and can use com-
    puters as a tool for inquiry, problem-solving,
    and recreation.
(8) The student values aesthetic components of com-
    puter science and computer applications.
(9) The student is confident of the right to devel-
    op, hold, or express conventional or unusual
    ideas related to computers and computer applica-
    tions.
(10) The student is able to adapt concepts and proc-
    esses of computer science to examine issues, to
    clarify personal values, to solve personal and
    social problems, and to satisfy personal curi-
    osity.
(11) The student knows and values ethical obligations
    and legal responsibilities related to computer
    use.
(12) The student values knowledge and skills related
    to computing which enable individuals and groups

to cope with the complexity of human society.
(13) The student is able to make responsible decisions about computer uses that affect the student's economic, political, physical or social environment.

IV
SOFTWARE
AVAILABILITY

INTRODUCTION

While CAI can be used in almost all school curricula its application can be as diversified as the
subjects it services. Educators working in humani-
ties and visual arts are developing software which
teach fundamental concepts, compose visual and poet-
ic forms, perform stylistic analyses and retrieve
information. There has been experimenting with new
hardware devices as creative media as well as for
research and instructional purposes.

Music educators are using the computer as a
pedagogical tool in music appreciation and history,
ear-training and discrimination, composition, funda-
mentals, and instructional methods.   Musical tones
can be produced singly or in combination for melodic
and harmonic dictation. Instructional management
systems have been developed, along with programs to
analyze musical forms, print music, and retrieve information. Computers are being used in the field of
dance to facilitate notation. Consideration is being given to computerized animation for training
dancers and studying choreography.

Using the computer's ability to provide repetition as required, to represent small, systematic
units of material, and to provide for immediate
feedback and individualized instruction make the

computer an attractive instructional aid in special education. It is in this field that effective instruction is carried out in small groups or on a one-to-one basis. This may be due, in part, to the special education population being heterogeneous in composition.

The computer by the advent of the microprocessor has assumed a relatively new role as that of a prosthetic device. Although many of these devices are still in the experimental stage, there is promise in eventually lessening the handicapping conditions of the deaf, blind and physically impaired. The largest handicapped group to benefit from computer technology has been the deaf. Another major group to benefit from CAI has been the developmentally disabled or mentally handicapped population, as well as the nonspeaking autistic children.

Some experimental work has been done using CAI with gifted children. While some educators have used it in an instructional mode, others find it more effective to allow the gifted to self-develop software for educational purposes.

In social studies, there is a need to provide students, with a laboratory experience which allows the student to conduct experiments, examine and analyze data or construct and examine models. The computers can help, too, in some of these areas by providing the student with an "environment" in which he/she can analyze data, construct and manipulate models, and test hypotheses. The problems of handling remedial training for students have increased, because the problems of bilingual and disadvantaged students and inadequate English and mathematics skills of entering university students are being recognized.

CAI can especially be used by the teacher of the regular classroom as an aid to the already existing curriculum. This could include such subject areas as art, business, language arts, mathematics, physical education, reading, and science.

SELECTION OF SOFTWARE

The past decade of instructional computing experience has convinced educators that the selection of the proper hardware for a classroom is only part of the job. The selection of quality software is of equal importance. Various sources of educational software now exist including hardware manufacturers, curriculum companies and software "clearing houses."

Most computer manufacturers such as APPLE, Texas Instruments, IBM, PET, Radio Shack, etc., provide software with their hardware. The larger companies in the computer business for a length of time such as Hewlett-Packard generally have a greater catalog of software, although the microcomputer companies are quickly catching up. Houghton-Mifflin and Computer Curriculum Corporation are two of the larger curriculum companies supplying educational software. Many of the larger publishing houses are also providing software to accompany the textbooks they sell.

After reviewing the instructional software available, the educator may discover the need for developing his/her own software for students to use. Many times, the readily available software does not meet the needs of all pupils. Some suggested guidelines are given here for the development and/or evaluation of quality instructional software.

QUALITY SOFTWARE GUIDELINES

As with any project development, analysis must come first. Deciding whether a particular idea is appropriate for the computer is very important and sometimes difficult to decide. An example of an inappropriate use of the computer is in using it as a "page turner" for pages of information. Presenting large amounts of information on screen after screen or page after page might just as effectively be accomplished on a printed ditto sheet.

Another example of misuse is to have the computer simulate a pendulum and then allow the students to change the variables of mass, period, and length. A much better learning experience might be to provide the student with string, paper clip, and some washers. Though we might even be able to draw a picture of the washer on the screen or printer of the computer, the actual washers and strings will provide a more complete and meaningful experience for the student. It is important that we do not try to "computerize" all learning situations.

To evaluate and/or design software, it is important to know the capabilities and limitations of the machine for which the software is intended. One must consider memory size, computational speed, abilities for visual display, and audio output. Many times, ideas do not have to be rejected, but modifications need to be made.

It is important to emphasize user interaction. Programs should be designed for active, not passive learners. They should allow students to point to things in the program, use supplementary resources, or type responses on the keyboard. Variety should be used for added interest.

The program should be exciting and rewarding. After a few experiences with the computer, the student soon learns what happens when they get a question wrong and what happens when they answer correctly. Many will deliberately answer questions incorrectly just to find out what happens. Reinforcement for a correct response should not be less motivational than the program's reaction to an incorrect response. For example, in a microcomputer version of hangman, the computer prints a boat on the screen. To the side, it prints the blanks for the number of letters in the word for which the computer is thinking. If an incorrect response is given, the boat sinks in the water. If enough incorrect letters are selected, a little man is seen going down in the water with bubbles coming from his mouth. This is very entertaining for the student--considering that he lost! A more positively motivational version would contain a similar happening providing the child is correct and less activity if incorrect.

The layout and design of the program is very important in a quality product. Like any curriculum material, instructional computing material must fit the existing curriculum and goals of the overall curriculum.

The display, whether on a screen or on a printer, can be overloaded if too much material is printed at one time. Such masses of information tend to bore the user and should be broken into smaller segments for more interesting lessons. Double spacing, instead of single spacing, also help alleviate these problems. Unless earphones are available, it is a good practice to avoid using most sound effects that might be available on some computers when programs are intended for individual users in a classroom. The sound may be distracting for others in the classroom. However, sound might be used to notify the teacher when a student needs help.

When using microcomputers, color is another added feature to consider. Its use can be an asset to the program if used properly. However, it is important to not make the student responses color-dependent without providing a color key on the screen. Different television screens show colors in varying shades. If the program is used on a black-and-white monitor, the colors will be shades of gray.

The proper use of reinforcers in a lesson is also an important aspect of a good program. An effective reinforcement technique is not to simply say "OK" but to give additional reinforcement such as "GOOD JOB!" or "GREAT!!!" or "THAT'S ABSOLUTELY CORRECT!" These responses, used in variety, can be more motivating to the student than the standard "CORRECT" or "O.K."

At the conclusion of a program it is important for the student to be given a report of how he/she has done on the lesson performed. Most students expect this type of feedback. This may be in the form of a score, a percent, or a message to move on to the next lesson. Also, some type of written record on which the students mark their own score may be useful.

V
COMPUTER APPLICATIONS FOR EDUCATIONAL ADMINISTRATION

INTRODUCTION

Computer technology is revolutionizing while improving the delivery and quality of educational services. Administrative processing has traditionally attended to the typical areas of students, personnel, financing, facilities and equipment, and curriculum. The procedures for implementing the majority of these functions have been adapted from business models.

These models have worked well for administrative tasks because of the large amounts of information to be processed and the kinds of repetitive operations needed to do so. A recent extension of these computational and clerical jobs includes a new array of administrative operations for educational management systems.

Advancements in meeting the needs specific to the educational administrator are resulting in enhanced decision-making procedures which include planning, budgeting, accountability, and so on. These new software systems are enabling administrative services to accomplish computer assisted modes of information control, reporting, operations research, feasibility simulations, modeling, and generally more efficient decision-making. These functions combined with the more traditional business, mathematical, and statistical computer applications have greatly expanded the potentials for integrating administrative needs and efficient student services.

STUDENT MASTER FILE

In a system where close coordination of student-oriented services is desired, it is essential that some sort of central data base be maintained. This base is usually known as a student master file. The data contained in such a file would include the student's name, current address, date of birth, grade level, current campus (and, perhaps, previous campuses), telephone number, parents' occupations and business address (needed for various federal reports occasionally), with such additional information as a particular district might desire. From this data base the various student services can be built. For instance, the generation of student directories would be a relatively easy task, and could be based on name, address, grade, or other criterion. In addition, the demographic data could serve to furnish information regarding bus routes, attendance areas, and similar census-type information.

Some computer systems allow continuous inquiry and update on the student master file, a capability which greatly enhances its use. Otherwise, the process of obtaining useful data would involve calling for a printout of all data at a remote location at an inconvenient time, or would involve updating at infrequent intervals, making a current file difficult to achieve.

A word regarding remote job entry is appropriate here. The process of gathering data for a certain computer run, with its attendant cards or tape input, and transporting that data to a distant computer center for processing has long been a familiar one, if unpleasant. For some types of services, the hand-carry method is the only way. For many routine

TABLE 5.1

AREAS OF ADMINISTRATIVE COMPUTER SERVICES

Class Scheduling	Helps schools develop master schedules by supplying a series of reports and summaries. enables master schedule to be adjusted repeatedly, reduces class course conflicts, minimizes problems caused by pupil changes and produces numerous reports for school management use.
Grade Reporting	Provides schools with computer produced report cards for students, provides schools with analysis of student grades through a cycle of semester summaries and reports. supplies schools with semester and year-end labels with grades and credits.
Attendance Accounting	Produces student attendance reports, supplies districts with analysis of attendance including breakouts of special education students, and provides bus data reports.
Test Scoring	Scoring service of standardized group tests which provides schools with appraisals of student levels of competence in the basic skill areas, diagnosis of learning difficulties, appraises gains and growth in achievement, aids instructional planning, assists in evaluating curriculum.
Payroll	Provides school districts with employee paychecks, procedures for changing of data, and special reports needed in payroll preparation.
Finance	Aids school districts in efficient collection, compiling and reporting of educational data. provides detailed records of all transactions, prints vendor checks by computer, provides audit trail while allowing school districts to classify their transactions in greater detail than would be feasible by manual methods.
Tax Accounting	Automation of a school district tax offices, maintains master file information on taxpayers in school district, computes current taxes based on assessment ratios and tax rates, prepares current tax statements, current tax receipts, notices, and other tax accounting information.
Inventory Accounting	Provides up to date information on the status of all fixed assets.
Classroom Test Scoring	Assists school teachers in correcting classroom tests.
Public Opinion Polling	Computerized opinion polling system which can be used in getting views of general or specific groups.
Media Retrieval	Allows teachers to request materials in any of several ways—by interest or grade level. subject. format. etc.—and produces a listing of what is available.

33

services, such as those mentioned above, and those yet to be covered, there is a better way. Certain systems allow a modified form of time-sharing. The CPU channels the work from a remote entry point (a card reader, tape reader, or similar input) located at a school or administrative office to the appropriate peripheral devices and processing areas, and then returns the output to (usually) a line printer located at the remote entry point. The remote user has at his/her disposal the entire computational and processing capability of the central system, and except for emergencies, has little need for contact with the computer center personnel. The savings of such an arrangement in terms of time and money contrasted with the costs of the terminal equipment are subject to several levels of analysis. For a large school system or group of districts, the remote entry arrangement is highly desirable and generally economically feasible. The costs would be difficult to justify for a small system or for an infrequent user. An alternative approach utilizes a mini-computer used locally for various tasks as a remote entry to a larger system capable of larger or more complex tasks than the minicomputer can handle. Compatibility of data form is essential, but various approaches to interfacing are available commercially.

A specific remote utilization is that in the counseling office of a school, where the counselor accesses a student's file and can make more meaningful decisions based on current data. Additionally, the counselor can update the file and allow others to have the most current information immediately.

CLASS ATTENDANCE

Most states have very specific guidelines regarding school attendance, and all affected school districts have the responsibility of complying with those guidelines. For example, certain state-level financial aid might be based on attendance information, and very rigid procedures would help standard-

ize the reporting. The computerization of some of
the reporting and recording tasks has helped the
large districts especially. Items regarding attendance are added to the student master file, either as
exact dates (or portions) absent or a cumulative
total to date. Periodic reports can be generated
for use by the school principal or district superin-
tendent, as the administrator analyzes the funding
situation or prepares an official report to a state
agency.

GRADING AND GRADE ANALYSIS

The speed at which a computer operates allows
application of computerized analysis to grades and
grading. Programs may be written or drawn from
software libraries to aid in statistical analysis,
such as central tendencies and skewing. Histograpic
or other representation of a set of grades aids sig-
nificantly in analyzing the effectiveness of testing
or the appropriateness of a grading procedure. Programs to make such representations are also available or are quickly developed. A teacher charged
with the responsibility of teaching the computer
mathematics area would be the natural choice for developing or implementing such teacher aids.

The attempt at universality with which every
software package is made usually falls short of specific applications. The "canned" programs are
usually good starting points, and with modification
can be made to work in a particular situation.

Depending upon the type of system available,
routine grade averaging may or may not be efficient-
ly handled on a computer. If a teacher has a microcomputer system available, its utilization should be
considered. If, however, a large system (batch or
timesharing) is utilized, the cost for simple grade
averaging would likely be high. A simple hand calculator might prove more efficient.

Using optical scanning techniques, most computer
centers provide for several test-scoring services.
If a test is set up with a multiple-choice format,
it can be graded rapidly, and the computer can imme-

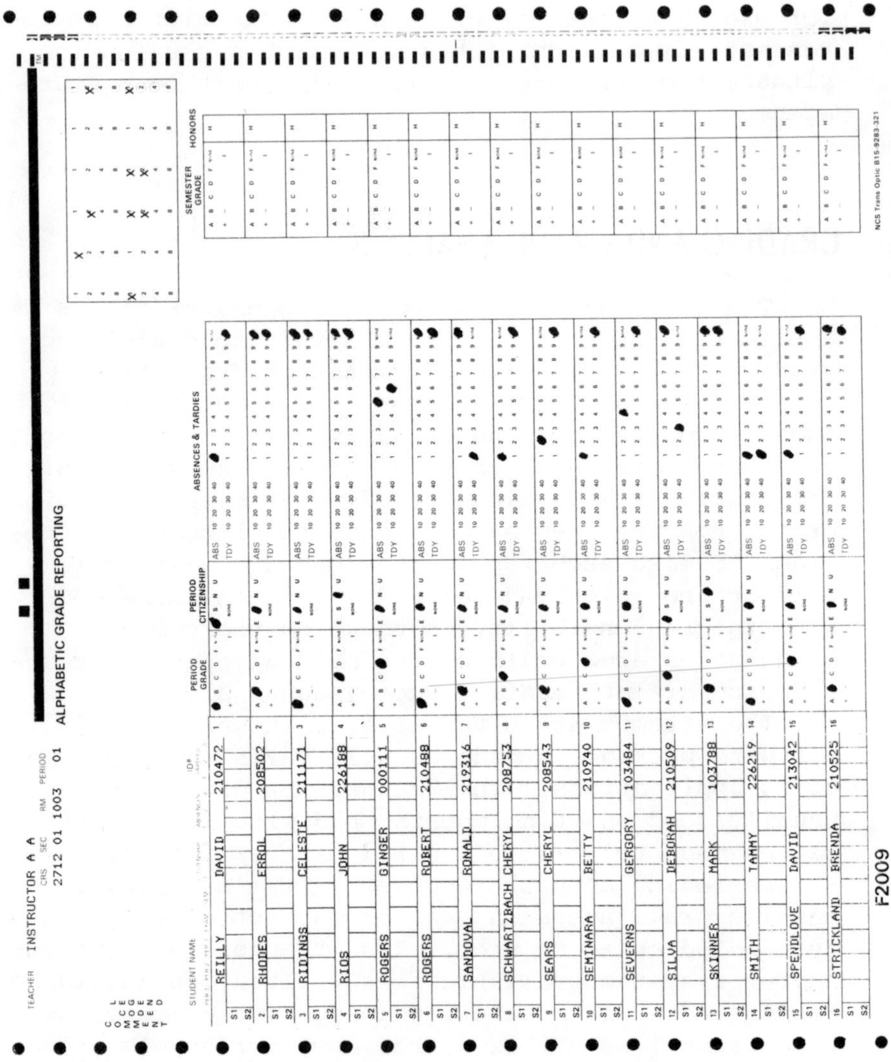

TEACHER INSTRUCTOR A A

CRS	SEC	RM	PERIOD
2712	01	1003	01

ALPHABETIC GRADE REPORTING

	STUDENT NAME		ID#
1	REILLY	DAVID	210472
2	RHODES	ERROL	208502
3	RIDINGS	CELESTE	211171
4	RIOS	JOHN	226188
5	ROGERS	GINGER	000111
6	ROGERS	ROBERT	210488
7	SANDOVAL	RONALD	219316
8	SCHWARTZBACH	CHERYL	208753
9	SEARS	CHERYL	208543
10	SEMINARA	BETTY	210940
11	SEVERNS	GERGORY	103484
12	SILVA	DEBORAH	210509
13	SKINNER	MARK	103788
14	SMITH	TAMMY	226219
15	SPENDLOVE	DAVID	213042
16	STRICKLAND	BRENDA	210525

PERIOD GRADE A B C D F NONE

PERIOD CITIZENSHIP E S N U NONE

ABSENCES & TARDIES ABS TDY 10 20 30 40 1 2 3 4 5 6 7 8 9 NONE

SEMESTER GRADE A B C D F NONE

HONORS H

F2009

NCS Trans Optic B15-9283-321

Figure 5.1. Grade Reporting Form.

diately generate several useful analyses. For example, a simple class roster with raw scores is a direct outcome; from this information, percentile ranks based on a single class, a group of classes, an entire school population, or based on national norms can be generated. A frequency distribution of the particular raw scores would be an additional measure of class response; a further statistical summary might include such things as: number of students who took each part of the test; number of questions in the particular part; division points for the four quartiles; mean score; and standard deviation and test reliability values. In order to judge the test itself, an item analysis is useful, which determines how many students answered each question correctly, how many chose each of the possible wrong answers, and how many omitted the item. With proper planning, this type of grading service can be utilized at many points during the school year, since the costs are usually quite low.

Figure 5.2. Optical Page Reader.

GRADE REPORTING

The automation of grade accounting and reporting is a great boon to both teacher and administrator. Grades may be recorded on mark-sense sheets or cards and then read into the system for later use. Once the data is stored, it can be recalled to generate a number of useful reports. The periodic issuance of report cards to parent and student is usually the first report. A proof report is usually sent to each teacher so that the computer's output can be checked against the intended input. Additional reports and analyses can be generated by grade level, subject area, name, pass/fail classification, or teacher, to allow more extended use of the grade information. The report cards and certain reports would be required for each grading cycle (for instance, every six or nine weeks), whereas summary reports and final status reports might be called for only once each school year.

SCHEDULING

The availability of computerized methods has greatly improved the situation of the principal and the counseling staff which required that they schedule students into reasonable accord with class size, room usage, and graduation requirements, not to mention student/parent course choices. Several software packages are available for this task, among them IBM's SOCRATES (Scheduling Of Classes Realized Automatically Through Effortless Systematization), which allows a very efficient application of administrative time in preparing input, producing useful and meaningful output in terms of conflicts, areas of possible conflict, areas of satisfactory scheduling, and building/teacher utilization. Once the initial outputs have been analyzed and conflicts resolved (to some extent), then schedules can be implemented and printed for distribution. This

process of scheduling and distribution of proposed
schedules should take place in the spring, so as to
allow further resolution of conflicts before the
fall term arrives and before schedule alteration becomes much more difficult. After the remaining conflicts are resolved as far as possible, final requests for schedules and relevant reports are made.
Tentative class rosters and teacher loads are made,
and information becomes available for all aspects of
the academic process. From these reports requests
for additional teaching personnel are made, as well
as for proper quantities of the correct textbooks
and other teaching supplies.

PAYROLL

Administrative areas which affect the student
but which are not directly involved with day-to-
day scholastic progress, are those associated with
financial and business aspects of the school district. These areas can be roughly segmented into
payroll and non-payroll matters. More is involved
with payroll than merely noting a correct salary,
writing a check, and tallying the total payroll
amount. Several categories of personnel each require different procedures for arriving at a correct
compensation. Weekly or bi-weekly pay periods exist
for part-time or hourly employees. Most professional personnel have a monthly pay period. For each,
there are numerous separate accountings for with-
holding tax, social security (where applicable), re-
tirement payments, credit union payments, dues to
various organizations, time worked (for hourly employees, including overtime), sick leave or vacation
time status, annuity payments, and other locally applicable items. Not only must an accurate accounting be made to the employee, but all appropriate
records must be made and kept for each individual
area of deduction for later audit and reporting (as
in the case for tax reporting). To accomplish all
of these tasks accurately, a file similar in content
to the student master file must be created for all
employees. Each pay period, the file is updated

ROOM NO	COURSE CODE	COURSE TITLE	SECT NO	SEM	PERDS FR TO	DAYS	INST NO	INSTRUCTOR NAME	ORIG SEAT	--ASSIGNED--- FLAG BOY GRL MNR
1005	1361	GEOMETRY I	0001	7	04-04	ALL	0005	TEACHER EE	5	
	1361	GEOMETRY 1	0002	7	05-05	ALL	0005	TEACHER EE	5	
	1461	TRIG/A GEOM I	0001	7	02-02	ALL	0005	TEACHER EE	5	
	1461	TRIG/A GEOM I	0002	7	03-03	ALL	0005	TEACHER EE	5	
	1462	TRIG/A GEOM IH	0001	7	01-01	ALL	0005	TEACHER EE	5	

TOTAL CLASSES   5   TOTAL MODULES   75   TOTAL STUDENTS

PERS	------SEMESTER 1------					------SEMESTER 2------					------SEMESTER 3------				
	M	T	W	R	F	M	T	W	R	F	M	T	W	R	F
01	X	X	X	X	X	X	X	X	X	X	X	X	X	X	X
02	X	X	X	X	X	X	X	X	X	X	X	X	X	X	X
03	X	X		X	X	X	X		X	X	X	X		X	X
04	X	X		X	X	X	X		X	X	X	X		X	X
05	X			X	X	X			X	X	X			X	X
06															
07															

PERCENT UTILIZATION   71.

Figure 5.3.   Room utilization Report.

40

with the new information regarding the current wages
and deductions.   Here again is an area where remote
inquiry and update is to be desired, as well as a
possible remote job entry.   Most computer centers
require that customers order and furnish their own
check stock, with the specifications to be in keeping with required guidelines for the equipment to be
used. Adding or deleting items on the check usually
costs more in check stock than in program modification costs, and such expenses must be weighed carefully against the anticipated gains in procedure.
As an example of a cost estimate for payroll services, consider a school district with 4000 employees
to be paid monthly.

   As possible cost figures, assume a fee of $0.25
per employee for setting up the payroll master file,
a fee of $0.20 per employee for periodic maintenance
or update, and a cost of $0.18 per check (for 48,000
checks per year) plus the cost of check stock. If
maintenance were carried out once each month, then
the costs might look like this:

Initialization of payroll file (one-time cost)
   4000 employees at $0.25 .... $ 1,000
Monthly maintenance of files
   4000 employees at $0.20 for 12 months   9,600
Monthly payroll checks
   4000 employees at $0.18 for 12 months   8,640
         (+ cost of check stock)   ————————
                                             $19,240

Considering the bookkeeping tasks accomplished by
the computer process, the high degree of accuracy to
be expected, and the convenience of handling, the
costs are well within reason. It would be a full-
time task for two or three employees to keep a constant vigil over payroll accounts of this magnitude
and to produce the checks, were those tasks to be
performed by hand. The use of the computer to do
the work frees those employees to do other less
mechanical work, work involving thought and reason,
unsuited for automated control.

NON-PAYROLL SERVICES

Non-payroll services include a variety of book-keeping and disbursement tasks. At least two constant inventories are usually kept by all school districts, fixed assets and expendable supplies. In the category of fixed asset determination come such items as buildings, furnishings, and instructional equipment. A categorization might begin like this for type of item:

```
1000   Office furniture
2000   Classroom furniture
3000   Buildings—Administration
4000   Buildings—Instructional
5000   Instructional Equipment
etc.
```

Subheadings under these categories indicating use might be:

```
100   Administrative
200   Vocational Education
300   Adult Education
etc.
```

Further subheadings might indicate departmentalization:

```
10   Mathematics Department
20   Physical Education Department
etc.
```

Such classification allows easy access by administrators to inquiry regarding the status of various assets at any time. Also, less perfunctory paperwork occurs when inquiry and update are remotely enabled, freeing employees to continue with other assigned tasks.

The remaining type of inventory is associated with expendable materials, including such items as janatorial supplies, lumber, paint, electrical supplies, spirit duplicator and mimeograph paper, textbooks, audio-visual equipment and supplies, and numerous other classifications. A computerized

STATEMENT OF DELINQUENT TAXES

ANYPLACE IND SCHOOL DISTRICT
AND
ANYCITY THREE

REAL ESTATE AND/OR PERSONAL PROPERTY TAX
09/25/80
DATE OF STATEMENT
REMIT TO:

NAME & ADDRESS: BEETHOVEN LUDWIG VAN   78212

U. R. WRIGHT
ANYPLACE IND SCHOOL DISTRICT
1973 REVENUE DRIVE
ANYPLACE, TEXAS 99999
PHONE: A/C 123 456-7890
RETURN THIS FORM WITH PAYMENT

PROPERTY DESCRIPTION: LT 12 BLK 26 CB 5833C HOLLYWOOD PARK UNIT 5

AMOUNT DUE INCLUDING PENALTY & INTEREST

YEAR	ORIGINAL TAX SCHOOL	CITY	TOTAL	IF PAID IN SEPTEMBER	IF PAID IN OCTOBER	IF PAID IN NOVEMBER	IF PAID IN DECEMBER
80	56.00	8.40	64.40	98.28	98.64	99.01	99.40
79	48.65	8.40	57.05	75.48	75.81	76.13	76.46
78	33.54	8.4C	41.94	58.92	59.14	59.40	59.64
77	33.54	8.40	41.94	61.81	62.05	62.30	62.52
76	41.64	19.95	61.59	94.08	94.42	94.78	95.13
74	49.14		49.14	81.25	81.52	81.81	82.10

PAY THIS AMOUNT: 469.82 | 471.58 | 473.43 | 475.25

SEE REVERSE SIDE FOR TABLE OF PENALTY & INTEREST

Figure 5.4.   Statement of Delinquent Taxes.

accounting system insures a closer control over status of supplies, lessens the time lag between the discovery of needs and the reordering of replacements, and lessens the physical problems involved in carrying out a frequent item-by-item physical inventory. Again the use of an on-line inquiry/update system is to be encouraged for inventory control.

The disbursement of funds to cover purchases and expenditures is similar in nature to the payroll system, in that computerized bookkeeping can be applied to the records, and the checks and reorders can be written directly from the computer on the line printer. An obvious application of on-line access to files is in the area of purchasing and accounts receivable. When payments for any receivable accounts are collected, they can be posted directly to the proper account; in the same manner, costs and other information can be entered to the proper account ledger by direct input. The current status of accounts aids greatly in determination of whether a given account is within budget guidelines, since each transaction has listed such items as source of materials, destination (for example, the math department of a particular high school), cost, quantities, etc., and inquiry can be based on any of these categories.

The listing above is by no means exhaustive, but it is representative of areas which can be served by a versatile computer system; in fact, as has been mentioned, most computer installations of any significant size can be pressed into service both as an educational aid in the classroom and as an adjunct to the administrative services of a school district. Awareness of these possibilities should allow a more knowledgeable approach to efficient computer system utilization.

ADMINISTRATIVE RECOMMENDATIONS

Computers have a tremendous potential to accomplish routine administrative tasks while improving educational services. Software specific to the needs of the educational administrator is most frequently available in association with on-line communications systems as opposed to the self-contained microcomputer. The initial costs and maintenance of on-line systems are considered to be "high" but continue to remain cost-efficient in the overall scheme of administrative processing. Funding for such equipment, however, will most assuredly need to come from within the District with possible vendor support. The trend in funding at the State and National levels has been continuously focused upon instructional projects since 1977.

The larger the student population which will be directly affected by the technology, the easier it is to justify the time, equipment, and funding needed to accomplish rapid and accurate information processing. The traditionally conservative educational community which for the sake of argument includes parents, must be informed of a specific rationale in order to accomplish such financing. The following comments may be useful in articulating such a rationale:

> "At a time when our nation is spending so much on education, the levels of understanding produced in students by that system appear lower each year. An answer may lie in educational technology in the form of the computer and in effective organizational and managerial techniques to apply this technology to the nation's schools." (October 1977--U.S. House of Representatives Committee on Science and Technology, "Computers and the Learning Society").

> "The humane and effective use of any technology requires a clear view of its role in meeting public needs and enhancing the well-being of our Nation and of the world community. By augmenting educational resources and improving services, information technology promotes the advancement of learning and of research in all fields." (April 1980--U.S. House of Representatives Joint Hearing and Workshop, "Information Technology in Education").

"At least two other important economic issues must be considered. One is the effect of information technology on the utilization of educational personnel, including the costs of appropriate training and the updating of skills. The second is the value of information technology in school management and administration; the flexibility of today's equipment offers the possibility of designing systems capable of performing concurrently both instructional and administrative tasks. Furthermore, the significance of such qualitative and quantitative trade-offs need to be viewed within the context of a more fundamental economic issue--the long-term effect on our national productivity of the widespread use of (or failure to use) information technology in education." (April 1980--U.S. House of Representatives Joint Hearing and Workshop, "Information Technology in Education").

And finally, the following statement which was the opening line on a recent letter from the Office of the Director, United States Department of Commerce, National Technical Information Services:

"The United States must find ways to increase industrial innovation or lose its position as the world leader in developing new products, new processes, and new technologies." (March 1980).

Educational applications of computer technology at any level of intent are socially, economically, and politically critical.

VI
EDUCATIONAL GAMES

INTRODUCTION

The computer has been increasingly used as an entertainment pastime on many campuses, supporting games such as "Football," "Startrek," etc. Too much game playing may cause burdens for the budget, but a certain amount of terminal usage that is gained by the use of games is important. There are other games associated with computers that can be great learning tools. MOVIN' ON, BINGO, I HAVE, and BUGS are all entertaining games that also are instructional. Hands-Up is a game that can easily demonstrate the operation of binary arithmetic, while Hexapawn gives the student an idea of how a computer "remembers." Another teaching aid discussed in this chapter, CARDIAC, is manufactured for sale. CARDIAC is designed to demonstrate the internal operation of a computer and is tremendously helpful when discussing programming.

MOVIN' ON

MOVIN' ON is a simple game used to reinforce topics in computing. One only needs a simple game board, cards (similar to a regular deck of cards)

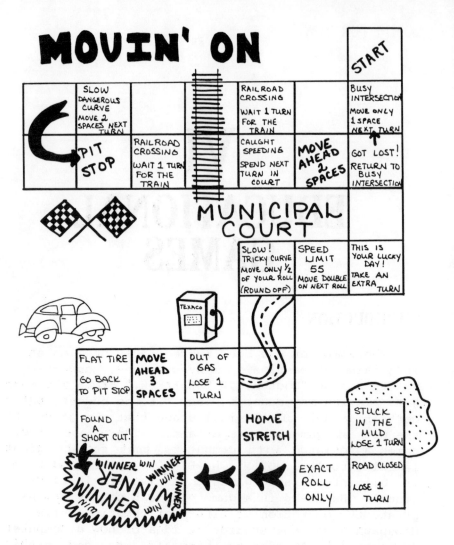

with a question on one side and the correct answer
on the other side, one die and four markers.

MOVIN' ON may be played by two to four players.
Each player in turn answers the questions or solves
the problem which is face up on the top of the deck.
The player then checks the correct answer on the
back of the card. If correct, the die is rolled and
the player's marker moved the number of spaces indicated. If incorrect, no move is made. The object
of the game is to be the first player to reach the
finish line.

COMPUTER BINGO

This version of the more standard BINGO is an excellent class game and may be used to strengthen vocabulary, reinforce learning or for review. A classroom set of COMPUTER BINGO cards, markers and a set of flash cards are needed.

Each student is given a card and a handful of markers. The caller holds the flash cards so that each may be seen. Players cover the figures found with markers. Play continues until a player has covered all of the spaces in a row, either horizontally, vertically or diagonally. The winner gets to call the next game. No need for prizes--it is fun to be the caller.

BINGO call cards and sample cards are shown.

COMPUTER BINGO CALL CARDS

1. CLEAR or HOME
2. BREAK or CNTRL C
3. Exponent Symbol
4. Cursor
5. ?
6. LOAD or CLOAD
7. Addition Symbol
8. Keyboard
9. C.R.T.
10. Software
11. RUN
12. Multiplication Symbol
13. Division Symbol
14. Back Space
15. String Variable
16. Forward Space
17. Greater or Equal

18. Not Equal

19. Less or Equal

20. Terminal Sign

21. Process Box

22. Hollerith

23. Input/Output Box

24. Connector

25. Decision Box

26. Subtraction Symbol

27. Babbage

28. ENTER or RETURN

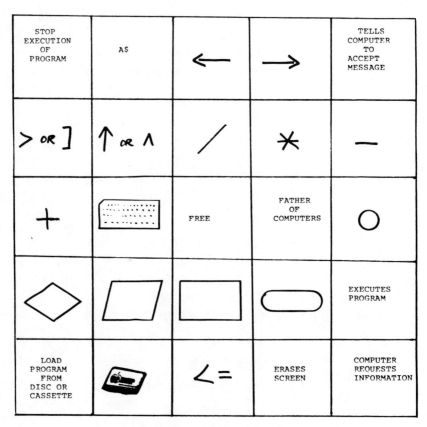

Sample Bingo Card

< >		O	+	>=
*	COMPUTER REQUESTS INFORMATION	←		TELLS COMPUTER TO ACCEPT MESSAGE
+	STOP EXECUTION OF PROGRAM	FREE	/	
> OR]		—	ERASES PROGRAM	→
	A$	FATHER OF COMPUTERS	↑ OR ∧	< =

Sample Bingo Card

I HAVE - WHO HAS

I HAVE—WHO HAS is intended for use in a total class setting and may be used in any subject or topic. Each student in the class is given only one card and must listen carefully so that he/she can

respond at the proper time. The card design is
shown below.

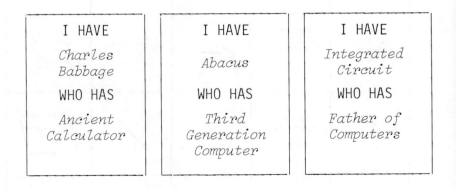

The cards are shuffled and dealt out to each
member of the class, one card per student until the
deck is exhausted. With a slower class, two cards
per student is more effective. Choose a student to
begin the activity. That student begins by reading
the top portion of the card, "I have [statement],"
he/she pauses and then reads the bottom portion of
the card, "Who has [question]." The student in the
class having the answer to the "Who has" question
at the top of his card responds by reading his entire card in the same manner until the first student
answers. Sample "I have" and "Who has" statements
follow:

	I HAVE	WHO HAS
1.	punch card	command word that tells the computer to accept input
2.	ENTER	first generation computer
3.	vacuum tube	computer language using math formulas
4.	Fortran	viedo screen
5.	CRT	$

6. String Variable	↑
7. Exponent symbol	Father of computers
8. Charles Babbage	flowchart symbol, oval shaped
9. terminal symbol	command word for putting programs into the computer
10. LOAD	ancient calculator
11. Abacus	third generation computer
12. integrated circuit	software
13. cassette tape	first programmer
14. Ada Lovelace	first commercial computer
15. UNIVAC	information given to the computer from outside source
16. input	standard form of memory
17. magnetic core	second generation computer
18. transistor	smallest amount of information that can be known
19. bit	Beginners All-purpose Symbolic Instructional Code
20. BASIC	process box
21. rectangle	part of the computer that stores information
22. memory	computer code
23. programming	common input device
24. keyboard	fourth generation computer
25. chip	first aid to counting
26. fingers	decision box
27. diamond	inventor of the first adding machine
28. Blaise Pascal	symbol that joins parts of a flowchart
29. connector	information given by the computer to the user
30. output	command word to execute program
31. RUN	diagram of a solution
32. flowchart	eight bits
33. byte	the physical parts of a computer
34. hardware	input/output symbol
35. parallelogram	Hollerith's invention

BUGS

BUGS is a game to improve on recognition of computer terms. Materials needed include a deck of 62 cards, 2 wild cards, and a set of unbreakable "bugs" (plastic spiders, animals, spoons or some-such). To start play, a quantity of bugs, one less than the number of players, are placed in the middle of a table. For example, 6 players would have 5 bugs on the table.

Each player is dealt 4 cards, face down. The remaining cards are placed face down in front of the dealer. The players now examine their cards. They should be looking for cards with equivalent answers. The dealer starts the game by drawing the top card from the facedown pile. He/she must then discard one card to the player on his/her left. Likewise, the player on the left picks up the dealer's discard and passes one card to the left.

Action is continuous. The dealer is constantly picking up one card from the face-down pile and then passing one card to the left. Each of the other players is constantly picking up one card from the right and passing one card to the player on the left. At no time in the game should any player have more than 4 cards.

Play continues until one player finally obtains 4 equivalent value cards. The 4 cards are placed face-up on the table and he/she quickly reaches out to grab one of the bugs.

This is the signal to the other players that they too can reach out for a bug. Being short one bug on the table, one of the players will end up without one. That player then earns the letter "B" in bug. If someone becomes too enthusiastic and is the first to grab a bug when not actually having 4 equivalent cards, he/she loses that round and earns a letter. Cards are then shuffled and the deal is passed to the next person to the left. The game continues until someone spells out "BUG." NOTE: This game tends to be NOISY!

BUGS

10 sets, 6 cards per set, 2 wild cards

SET 1:
Basic
Fortran
Cobol
Ada
P1/1
Pascal

SET 2:
A$
C$
String Variable
FG$
XY$
String Variable

SET 3:
CRT
Output Device
Picture of TV
Printer
Video Screen
Cathode Ray Tube

SET 4:
Input Devices
Keyboard
Card Reader
Disc Drive
Picture: Keyboard
Picture: Cassette
   Recorder

SET 5:
Disc
Software
Tape
Punch Card
Workbook
Programs

SET 6:
Punch Card
Hollerith
Picture: Punch Card
Input Device
Software
Storage Device

SET 7:
Leaders in Computing
Charles Babbage
Herman Hollerith
Ada Lovelace
Blaise Pascal
Charles Babbage

SET 8:
Characteristics of Computer
   Generations
Chips
Integrated Circuits
Transistors
Vacuum Tubes
Bubble/Laser

SET 9:
Flowchart Symbols
Terminal Symbol
Decision Box
Process Box
Input/Output Symbol
Connector

SET 10:
Flowchart Symbols
Diagrams:
   Process Box
   Input/Output Symbol
   Decision Box
   Terminal Symbol
   Connector

HANDS-UP

Hands-Up is a simple game which may be used to demonstrate binary counting, addition, complement subtraction, and shifting. The game is played by having several students, representing a computer word, stand side by side facing the class. If a chalk-board is available for the students to stand in front of, it would be helpful to label each place 2^4, 2^3, 2^2, 2^1, 2^0, etc. There are two positions, or states, that each player may assume. These states are:

 "Hands up" denoting one, and "Hands down" denoting zero.

All players start in the zero state (hands down) and remain in that state until tapped on the shoulder. Once tapped, they must change state, or raise hands. For every tap thereafter, the player must change state. When a player in the one state is tapped, the hand is lowered to the zero state, tapping the next higher power of two on the shoulder.

To count, the players make a row, standing about one foot apart and facing the class. Another player, designated the "switch," stands near the player representing 2 :

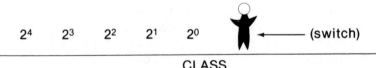

2^4 2^3 2^2 2^1 2^0 ←——— (switch)

CLASS

To begin, the switch taps the shoulder of 2^0 who, because he/she was in the zero state, must change states or raise his/her hand to represent one. The switch touches 2^0 again, so 2^0 must change states again, or lower his/her hand, tapping the shoulder of 2^1 on the way down. Then 2^1 must change states. Each time the switch taps 2^0, a chain reaction is created, causing the players to raise and lower their hands according to whether or not they are tapped. The resulting display of hands up and hands down will represent the number of times the switch has tapped 2^0 on the shoulder. For example:

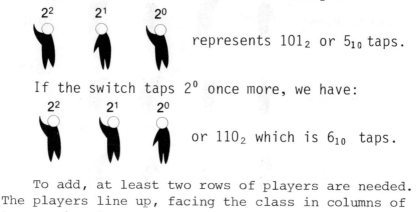

2^2 2^1 2^0

represents 101_2 or 5_{10} taps.

If the switch taps 2^0 once more, we have:

2^2 2^1 2^0

or 110_2 which is 6_{10} taps.

To add, at least two rows of players are needed. The players line up, facing the class in columns of two, each column representing a power of two:

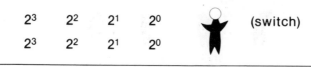

| 2^3 | 2^2 | 2^1 | 2^0 | | (switch) |
| 2^3 | 2^2 | 2^1 | 2^0 | | |

CLASS

Each row represents an addend, so the players must be put in a one or zero state (depending on the addend desired) before the addition takes place. When each row represents the numbers to be added, the switch gives a signal to begin. The players that are on the back row and in a one state tap the players immediately in front of them, causing those players to change state. If a person on the front row is in a one state when tapped, he/she taps the person to the next higher power in that row as he/she changes state. This indicates a carry into the next column. It is common for a player to be tapped from behind and from the side. This player must change states twice, leaving him/her in the original position, but causing a carry into the next column (because the next higher power was tapped during one of the changes of state). When addition is completed, the front row will represent the sum.

Example of Addition: add 0011_2 to 0101_2:

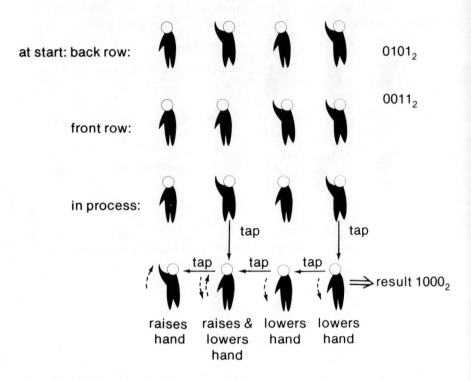

at start: back row: 0101_2

0011_2

front row:

in process:

tap   tap

tap   tap   tap   ⟹ result 1000_2

raises   raises &   lowers   lowers
hand   lowers   hand   hand
           hand

Complement arithmetic may be achieved as follows: Players line up as for addition, the front row being the number to be complemented or the number to be subtracted from the back row.   On a signal from the switch, everyone in the front row simply changes state forming the one's complement.   Then the switch taps the front row 2^0 to add one to the complement, resulting in the two's complement form of the original number.   The switch then signals the back row to begin addition as described above.   When completed, the front row will represent the difference.

To shift, only one row of players is needed. For a circular shift on a signal from the switch, everyone changes to the state of the person representing the next lower power of two, while 2^0 assumes the state of the highest power of two displayed.   For example:

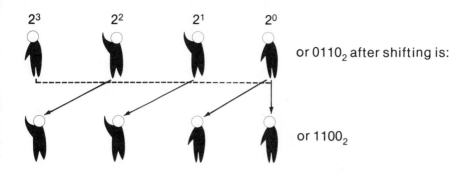

or 0110_2 after shifting is:

or 1100_2

HEXAPAWN

Hexapawn is a game which demonstrates how a computer improves its ability to play games by modifying its strategy according to past experience.   The game may also be used to demonstrate storage and removal of instructions from memory.

The playing board is divided into nine squares, similar to a tic-tac-toe board.   Each player has three markers which are placed in the squares nearest him, as so:

A move can be made in one of two ways:

(1) By moving a marker straight forward one square into an empty square.   If the square is occupied, no straight forward move may be made into this square, thus a block is achieved.

(2) By moving diagonally left or right into a square occupied by the opponent's marker, thus achieving a capture of this marker.

Note that a straight forward move is only allowed into an empty square.   A diagonal move is

only allowed into an occupied square. These are the
same as pawn moves in chess except that no double
move is permitted.

Examples:

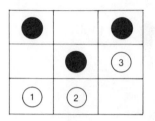

marker 1 may move straight forward
markers 2 and 3 are blocked

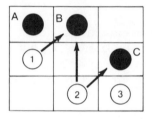

markers A and 3 are blocked
marker 1 may capture B by a diagonal
   move
marker 2 can move straight forward *or*
diagonally to capture C

A player tries to defeat "the computer" which is
actually a set of 24 matchboxes that bear diagrams
of all possible game situations. The diagrams show
the marker arrangement on the board and have colored
arrows which indicate all possible moves "the computer" could make in that particular situation. Only
the left end moves are considered because an opening
move on the right would lead to identical, although
mirror-reflected, lines of play. Inside each matchbox there is one colored bead corresponding to each
colored arrow on the diagram.

Players alternate moves, moving one marker at a
time. The computer always makes the second move.
The game is won in any of three ways:
(1) By advancing one marker to the third row:

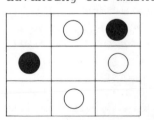

"◯" won

(2) By capturing all three of the opponent's markers:

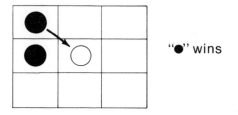

"●" wins

(3) By achieving a position in which the opponent cannot move (i.e. blocking all markers on the board):

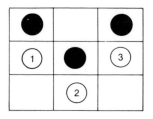

"○" won (assuming "●" are the computer's markers)

When it is the computer's turn to move, the player selects the matchbox which bears the diagram of the marker arrangement on the board. A colored bead is selected at random from this box and the move corresponding to that color arrow is made (an instruction is removed from memory). If the computer eventually wins that game, all the beads are put back in the matchboxes (instructions returned to memory). If the computer loses, all the beads except the last one extracted are replaced, thus the computer modifies its strategy and will never again make that losing move.

If in the course of play an empty box is found, there is no move the computer can make without losing, so the bead from the preceding move is not replaced when the next game begins.

The games are continued until eventually the computer has "weeded out" all of its losing moves and begins to win every time.

Example:

Computer

START

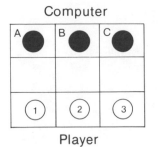

Player

Move #

(1)

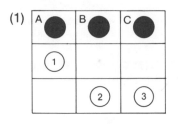

Player moves marker 1 straight ahead.
This situation pattern is found on matchbox.

(2)

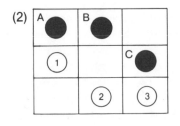

Bead ☐1 drawn indicates a straight forward move by C.

(3)

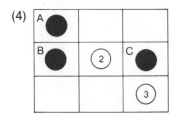

Player moves marker 2 straight forward.
This situation is found on matchbox.

(4)

Bead ☐2 drawn indicates a diagonal capture of marker 1 by marker B.

(5)

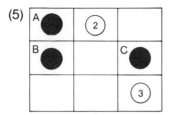

Player moves marker 2 straight forward
to the third row to win the game.

Since the player won, bead ☒ is not replaced, but bead ☐ is replaced
and another game begins.

The following illustration shows the design of
the necessary matchboxes, with the numbers on each
referring to the moves available to the computer at
the second, fourth and sixth move. In practice,
each arrow should be of a different color, with
matching colored beads inside.

2	2	4	4	4	4

4	4	4	4	4	4

4	6	6	6	6	6

6	6	6	6	6	6

Labels for Matchboxes

63

CARDIAC

CARDIAC (Cardboard Illustrative Aid to Computation) was developed by the Bell System. It was designed to help in understanding computers and can be an effective visual aid when teaching computer science. CARDIAC shows how a computer operates (even though it is made out of cardboard) in a way that is not necessarily observable even on a real computer. CARDIAC should be understandable to most high school students taking computer science. It consists of input, output, memory, an accumulator, program counter, and instruction register.

Input consists of a cardboard strip divided into boxes; each box can represent a punched card or line on a teletype. One number per box is entered on the strip. At the beginning of execution of the program, box 1 should appear in an input window. The instruction decoder will tell when to advance the input strip to the next box.

Output also consists of a cardboard strip, each box representing one line of output. At the beginning of execution of the program, the output strip should be blank. During execution of the program, the control section will direct the flow of output to the strip. Also what to put on the strip will be computed during the program.

Memory consists of three-digit decimal numbers. These numbers can be data or instructions, depending on how they are used. They must be entered and retrieved by the user.

The accumulator is the arithmetic unit. The user must keep track of the accumulator separately and must also set the accumulator test slide so that it agrees with the sign in the accumulator. The instruction decoder will give the instructions as to what to do to the accumulator and when.

The program counter is a pointer which keeps track of which instruction is to be executed next. Usually the value increases by one to be the address of the next cell. In some cases, however, the instruction register will call for an address out of

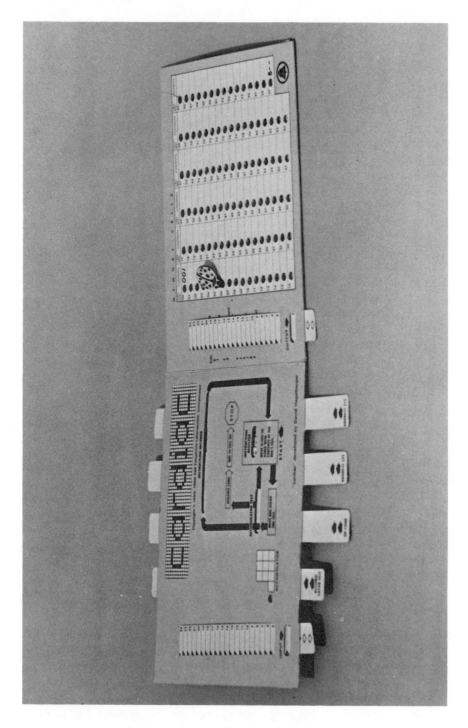

Figure 6.2.   CARDIAC.

65

sequence, so the program counter is resettable. The program counter is an arrow and must be moved by the user.

The instruction register contains the program word most recently fetched from the memory cells and is also a three-digit number. The first digit is the operational code and the last two are the address in memory to be operated on. The instruction decoder tells what to do for each operational code. The accumulator test is used to test the sign of the accumulator. It also tests input to see if the last box has been read.

The control unit follows a three-part cycle. First, it fetches an instruction from memory for the instruction register. Second, it increments the address in the program counter, making it the address of the next instruction. Finally, it makes the instruction register execute the instruction it contains. Throughout the operation, the user is the control unit.

OPERATIONAL CODES

Codes	Abbr.	Meaning
0AA	INP	Input. Copy input card into cell AA, advance input card.
1BB	CLA	Clear and add. Erase accumulator, copy contents of cell BB into accumulator.
2CC	ADD	Add contents of cell CC into accumulator.
3DD	TAC	Test accumulator contents. Move PC to cell DD if accumulator sign is negative, otherwise go to the next instruction.
4EF	SFT	Shift accumulator left E places, then right F places. When shifting, always fill with zeros.
5GG	OUT	Output. Copy contents of cell GG on output card, advance output card.
6HH	STO	Store. Copy accumulator into cell HH.
7II	SUB	Subtract contents of cell II from accumulator.
8JJ	JMP	Jump. Write PC cell number in last memory cell, move PC to cell JJ.

9KK   HRS   Halt and reset.   Move PC to cell KK
               and stop. Usually cell KK is cell
               00.

Examples of Programs.

Program #1. Add A to B to get sum S.

Address	Contents	Comments
07	016	Read A
08	017	Read B
09	116	Clear accumulator and add A
10	217	Add B (S is now in accumulator)
11	618	Store S
12	518	Print S
13	900	Halt and reset

To execute the program.

Write the program words in the indicated memory
   cells.
Write the two numbers on the input strip in cells
   1 and 2. Use two numbers whose sum will not ex-
   ceed 999. Reset the input strip to 1.
Put the program counter on cell 07.
Set the output strip to 1.
Follow program.

Program #2. Counting program with loop.

Address	Contents	Comments
11	100	Clear and add contents of cell 00.
12	603	Store contents of accumulator in cell 03.
13	503	Print contents of cell 03.
14	200	Add contents of cell 00.
15	812	Jump to instruction in cell 12.

This program has an unconditional jump and has no
way of getting out of the loop.

Program #3. Countdown from -4 to 0.

Address	Contents	Comments
00	+001	Data.
09	-004	Data.

67

10	109	-004 to accumulator.
11	200	Add 001.
12	608	Store accumulator in cell 08.
13	508	Print contents of cell 08.
14	311	Test accumulator. If minus, jump to cell 11. If plus, go ahead to cell 15.
15	900	Halt and reset.

Program #4. Multiplication by a single-digit multiplier. Multiplier A times multiplicand BC.

Address	Contents	Comments
06	001	Read BC into cell 01.
07	404	Clear acc.
08	602	Store acc. in cell 02. Clearing cell 02 for future storage of sum.
09	003	Read A into cell 03.
10	103	'n' to acc.
11	700	Subtract 1 from 'n'.
12	603	Store revised 'n'.
13	318	Test acc. sign.
14	102	Clear acc. Enter contents of cell 02.
15	201	Add BC to acc.
16	602	Store revised sum in cell 02.
17	810	Jump back to cell 10.
18	502	Print (product of A times BC).
19	900	Halt and reset.

References

1. Gardner, Martin. "Mathematical Games," Scientific American, March 1962.
2. CARDIAC is a Bell Systems Teaching Aid and is available commercially from AMF Electrical Products, Development Division, 1025 N. Royal St., Alexandria, Virginia, 22314.

VII
CURRENT TRENDS

INTRODUCTION

As predictions about future promise for computers in learning environments are ventured, it must be remembered that at best, the past is an incomplete guide to the future. The educator must look forward to new technology blended with the knowledge and the capabilities of the large scale equipment that has been primarily used in the past. The vast majority of educational uses of computers in recent years have employed large timesharing systems.

There is a strong indication, however, that the microcomputer, used by a single person at a time (or, at most, a small group of people), will be the focus of future educational activities. It is believed that the microcomputer which may on occasion be connected to another system (another microcomputer or perhaps a minicomputer) will become the major educational delivery system in the foreseeable future.

INTEGRATED SYSTEM DESIGN

The school of the 80s will be one utilizing microcomputers for instruction and teacher-related administrative functions and a larger computer system for general administrative functions. This "larger" system may be a minicomputer for the small to medium size school district or a connection to a regional service center's timesharing system.

Microcomputers will be utilized for three primary functions:

(1) Computer Assisted Instruction
(2) Instruction about computers (computer programming, computer literacy, etc.)
(3) Classroom administrative functions.

CAI will be implemented throughout educational systems. Most publishers now have textbooks that utilize supplemental CAI materials. Even though most educators now realize that the computer cannot and should not replace the teacher, most also realize the CAI provides an alternate mode of instruction that supplements and enhances regular classroom instruction and improves on the quality of instruction for our students. Microcomputers provide the most economical approach to providing hardware for CAI in the classroom.

Computer literacy is a topic of instruction that will be commonly introduced in school curriculum during the 80s. The microcomputer will be the most widely used computer system for this instruction.

With the microcomputer soon to be so readily available in the classroom, teachers will rightfully wish to utilize this system for "teacher related" administrative functions such as attendance, accounting, registrations, etc. The microcomputer will be used as an "intelligent" terminal for editing and formating before transferring data to the central timesharing system.

Two major problems faced by education systems using microcomputers are how to share programs from one site to another and how to provide printed output. One possible solution is microcomputer "net-

working." Here a central microcomputer system or
larger timesharing system could be used as a reposi-
tory of software applications which users could
download to their microcomputers. Having a centralized process aids users in two ways. Standardization of program versions can be monitored, insuring
that documentation produced is applicable to all
user groups. Also, user contributions to the central library of programs are easily transferred and
group quality review of such contributions can be
accomplished without needing individual copies for
each reviewer.

A microcomputer used as an "intelligent terminal" in a network could perform the less rigorous
processing requirements, thus freeing the central
computer's resources for larger tasks. The micro
could perform functions without calling on the network for help. The user's microcomputer could also
give him or her local calculator capabilities separate from the program being run. Benefits resulting from this kind of arrangement would include
faster response time (for those tasks processed
locally by microcomputers) and printed output of
programs uploaded to the central computer.

A perhaps unmeasurable, but extremely valuable
feature of using a microcomputer network to provide
service to school users at dispersed sites is the
ability of users to communicate with each other
using some type of "mailbox" program. While non-
intelligent terminals are satisfactory for sending
and receiving messages with such a program, the use
of microcomputers on a network could add word processing capabilities to the system. While school
correspondence does not require the features of a
business word processing system, the microcomputer
could give them easy memo format, paragraph setting,
and editing features.

Each classroom in the school would contain a
microcomputer with connection capabilities to the
central microcomputer or timesharing system. In
order to provide access to multiple microcomputer
systems for an entire class, a cluster of such systems should be available in a centralized laboratory
setting.

A common method for cutting network communica-

71

tion costs is to use a line sharing strategy. However, this adds the cost of new communications equipment. Microcomputers in the school could act as communications processing devices even as they handle stand alone applications for students. A microcomputer in school "A" could handle the transmissions of itself and the terminals in schools "B" and "C", thus replacing the needs for lines from all three sites to the central computer center.

The dominance of the telephone line as a communications medium will be challenged in the 1980s by other systems such as cable television. Cable systems can carry digital data signals as well as video. If schools in an area decide that use of a community cable TV network is less expensive for timesharing communications than phone lines, the microcomputer's intelligence could allow it to be programmed for cable capability.

MICROCOMPUTER LABORATORY

A microcomputer in every classroom will handle many of the day-to-day types of computing needs. However, the school of the future will have the need for a centralized laboratory for large class computer access. The remaining sections of this chapter represent a basic guide to the establishment of a computer laboratory using equipment and materials readily available in most schools' regular building inventory. Included are step-by-step directions for actual set up of the lab, suggested plans for the physical layout, suggestions for different centers and their uses, and a sampling of bulletin boards and posters. Barson, Morlan, and other sources listed in the Bibliography provide additional valuable information.

The establishment of a computer laboratory should be made in deliberate stages so that it may serve each student as he/she is guided through application to understanding and appreciation of each subject area. The instructional method used in the laboratory should not duplicate the classroom teacher's approach or materials. The methods and materials used should add a new dimension to learning.

The following represent the stages necessary in setting up a microcomputer laboratory:

STAGE ONE: <u>Consultation and analysis</u> regarding the role and objectives through conferences with school administrators and faculty. The selection of the microcomputer to be utilized should be this group's primary concern. Types of sessions and learning centers should be developed during this initial stage.

STAGE TWO: <u>Collecting and taking inventory</u> of all materials in the school that are potential laboratory items. All items should be catalogued and classified according to use and/or subject area and grade level. Check individual classrooms, teacher's lounge, department storage areas, book-rooms, and workrooms for basic furniture items not currently being used. Keep an eye out for desks and chairs, bookcases and shelves, tables suitable for game playing, storage closets, file cabinets, bulletin boards, overhead projector, screen. Drama department backdrops may be "stored" in the lab, as they make excellent partitions between centers!

STAGE THREE: <u>Design preliminary floor plan</u> for the laboratory. Take measurement of the room to be converted into the computer laboratory, making note of window and door openings, location of electrical outlets, and any unmoveable equipment in the room. It must be remembered that more space per square foot per student will be necessary in the labora-tory than in the regular classroom. The lab should have no more than the essential furnishings, for students prefer playing games on the floor, and standing while performing experiments. Additional electrical wiring may be required for the micro-computer system to be installed.

STAGE FOUR: <u>Limited purchases</u> are made based on the needs of the students to be served and the bare necessities found lacking. How much money? How much space? How many teachers? How many parapro-fessionals? How many students? are questions that need to be answered before any purchases are made.

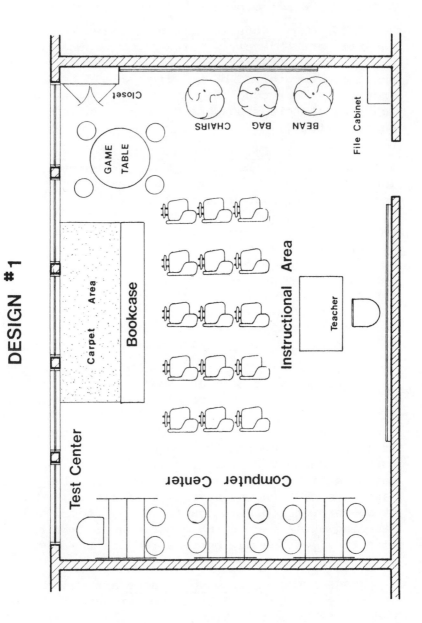

Figure 7.1. Microcomputer Laboratory Design # 1.

74

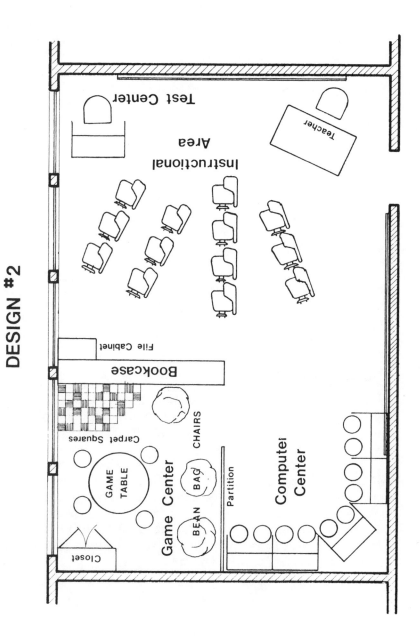

Figure 7.2.   Microcomputer Laboratory Design #2.

75

Individual carrels may be purchased to accommodate the microcomputers if desired. The various types of carrels should be studied before purchase to determine which style best suits the needs of the laboratory. Plastic dishpans from the local discount store make excellent storage bins and cost much less than commercial ones!! Collect empty boxes that will accommodate letter-size file folders. These may be modified and covered with self-adhesive paper to make inexpensive but attractive file boxes. Carpeting the game center lowers the noise level in the lab and decreases the number of tables and chairs needed. Carpet squares may be obtained from a local vendor at a nominal cost (usually free!!). These are especially nice as they may be stacked out of the way when not in use. Bean bag chairs are a luxury item that may be picked up at garage sales, salvage centers, or bargain basements!

STAGE FIVE: Implementation of the laboratory. Students of all ability levels should be included in the laboratory program. Students must be taught procedures for entering and leaving the lab, reading the schedule, locating materials, using equipment, attacking assignments, recording results, and handling completed assignments. Introduction to the laboratory approach should be initiated through group instruction before students are assigned to work in small groups or in pairs in order to free each of them to trust their own judgment. Teachers must be wary of the temptation to provide excessive direction. Scheduling use of the laboratory should be daily when possible. Teacher scheduling will depend upon different situations at individual schools. Time spent in the laboratory must be flexible. It should be determined by the student's ability and prescribed assignment. A sample student laboratory record sheet is shown in Figure 7.3.

STAGE SIX: The follow-up stage in the development of the lab is a gradual and on-going one in which, over a period of months or years, while the laboratory is in full operation, the teacher notes the equipment and materials essential to the improvement of the program.

COMPUTER LABORATORY CENTERS

The computer laboratory should be more than just a room with computers in it. An organization allowing various instructional centers is suggested. The arrangement of these centers should reflect teaching techniques geared to the learning style, creativity, and subject understanding, as well as the chronological age of the students served.

The teacher center is designed and equipped for testing, diagnosis, initial instruction of new concepts, reteaching, and conference. Overhead projector, screen, file cabinets, and chalkboard are preferred equipment.

The manipulative and game center is designed to contain concrete materials, kits, games, bookcases and/or cabinets, with ample workspace and floorspace. All materials should have directions to aid the students in completing their assigned tasks. Rules for games should be pasted to the boxes or gameboards.

The practice center is designed for pencil and paper activities such as worksheets, drill activities, and calculators. This may be near or incorporated into the teacher center.

The computer center is designed for the microcomputers set up in individual carrels. All instructions should be clearly posted so that the student may easily interact with the microcomputer. Any software necessary for completion of an assignment should be clearly marked and easily accessible.

The enrichment/project/testing center is designed for independent creative extensions of subject area concepts. Carrels are excellent for this. Students may also be sent here for makeup testing or assignments.

STUDENT LABORATORY RECORD

NAME _____

PERIOD _____

TEACHER _____

DATE	LESSON NO.	% COMPLETED	GRADE

Figure 7.3.   Sample Student Laboratory
Record Sheet.

ROLE OF THE LABORATORY TEACHER

The responsibility of the laboratory might be assigned to only one individual (similar to a library setup) or this responsibility may be shared by several. In any case, the following list of responsibilities should be considered.

1. Confer with the principal as to the role of the laboratory in the school.
2. Select items to be purchased for the lab and know how to provide maintenance for hardware.
3. Explore instructional potential of each commercial item as it is received.
4. Set up cross index of contents of commercial materials by concepts.
5. Prepare packets of relevant problem-solving situations.
6. Modify assignments using commercial kits to adapt to multi-level use.
7. Design open-ended assignments to enable students to display their strong points.
8. Develop a variety of teaching techniques to enable each student to learn in ways in which he/she learns best.
9. Assemble ample equipment and material for all students and/or centers.
10. Arrange the laboratory so students may move freely without interfering with one another.
11. Allow adequate work area--include floor space.
12. Provide laboratory orientation for students and faculty; initial visit.
13. Instruct students regarding the proper handling of equipment.
14. Show students where to find materials.
15. Maintain additional challenging assignments for students who complete their work before the end of the period.
16. Confer with students and teachers.

Master's Program In Nursing

SELECTING A MICROCOMPUTER

In selecting a microcomputer for instructional use, several questions and criteria should be considered. These include:

1. <u>Cost</u>. Consider the initial cost as well as the maintenance cost throughout the life of the system.

2. <u>Documentation</u>. Look for readable, well-sequenced, and complete instructions for the system and languages.

3. <u>Ease of Use</u>. Is the system too limited or too difficult? Is it portable? Is the system's arrangement or procedures acceptable? Can the output be easily read? Is the system susceptible to electrical interference?

4. <u>Programming Languages Available</u>. Does the system offer a variety of languages?

5. <u>Programs Available</u>. How many programs for the system are likely to be available? Are the present programs worth the price?

6. <u>Reliability</u>. How rugged is the system? How sturdy is the keyboard? How long is the equipment expected to last? Can the system withstand power surge or power failure? What is the quality of the cassette or disc? How often does the system have trouble loading or saving?

7. <u>Service</u>. How fast is the service? Is it local or sent away? Is it competent? What is the cost of servicing?

8. <u>Speed of Equipment</u>. How fast is the system as compared to other systems? Is the speed important? How fast do the peripherals work?

9. <u>Upward Compatibility</u>. Is the system expandable? How much will expansion cost?

SUPPLEMENTARY LABORATORY ACTIVITIES

No computer laboratory would be complete without supplementary activities. Included in this section are suggested bulletin board ideas and posters.

Take a LOOK
Around...

Leave power on!

Watch for electrical cords!

Put everything in its place!

Push chairs in!

All litter goes in the trashcan!

HELP???

Check these Clues

Did you press ENTER key?

Is your response correctly spelled?

Is your response correctly typed?

More than one response needed?

See Teacher!!

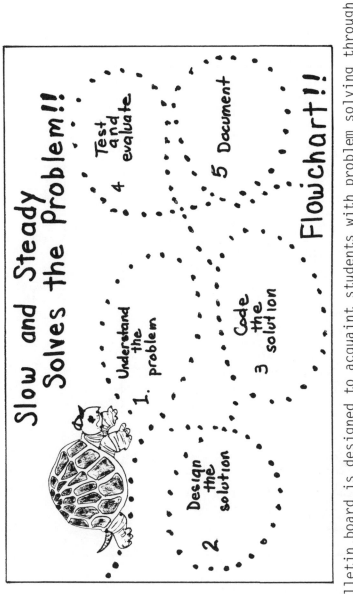

Slow and Steady Solves the Problem!!

1. Understand the problem
2. Design the solution
3. Code the solution
4. Test and evaluate
5. Document

Flowchart!!

This bulletin board is designed to acquaint students with problem solving through flow-charting. The turtle guides students through the five steps in flowcharting along a path of construction paper dots stapled to a kraft paper background. Numerals and letters are rendered with a felt marker directly onto the background paper. Caption and turtle are cut from tagboard and painted or colored.

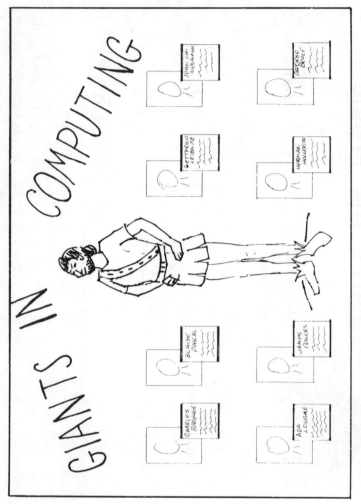

GIANTS IN COMPUTING

CHARLES BABBAGE

BLAISE PASCAL

GOTTFRIED LEIBNITZ

JOHN VON NEUMANN

ADA LOVELACE

JAMES POWERS

HERMAN HOLLERITH

GEORGE BOOLE

SUGGESTED BULLETIN BOARD: A bright yellow background with an enormous green giant centered on the board emphasizes the magnificent achievements of the people in the reports. Brief written reports on outstanding men and women in computing may be assigned, then displayed on the board.

BIBLIOGRAPHY

ACM Elementary and Secondary Schools Subcommittee. ES^3 Report. (Report). University of Oregon, Eugene, Oregon, 97403, February 1980.

Apple Computer Inc., Apple, the Personal Computer Magazine and Catalog. Regis Mckenna Publications, Palo Alto, California, 1979.

Barson, Alan, "The Mathematics Laboratory for the Elementary and Middle School," The Arithmetic Teacher, vol. 18, no. 8, NCTM, December, 1971.

"Computer Assisted Instruction: Current Trends and Critical Issues," Communications of the ACM (periodic news source). Published by the Association of Computing Machinery, vol. 23, no. 6, June 1980.

Computer Curriculum Corporation. Curriculum for Computer-Assisted Instruction (Pamphlet), 700 Hansen Way, Palo Alto, California 94303.

Control Data Education Company. Introduction to the PLATO System. (Report). Control Data Corporation, P.O. Box 0, Minneapolis, Minnesota 55440, 1980.

Educational Data Center. Information Systems for Schools. 100 DeLasalle Drive, Lockport, Illinois 60441, 1980.

Educational Facilities Laboratories, "Instructional Hardware," Report, 1970.

Houston Independent School District, Handbook for Creating a Mathematics Laboratory, H.I.S.D. Department of Curriculum.

International Business Machines Corporation. Academic Processing at Huntington Beach Union High School District, California (Application Brief GK20-1296-0 (2/80)). Data Processing Division,

1133 Westchester Avenue, White Plains, New York
10604.

Issacson, Dan. Discover the Microcomputer as an Instructional Media Tool in Elementary and Secondary Teaching: A Laboratory for In-Service and
Pre-Service Teachers. (Report). University of
Oregon, Eugene, Oregon 97403, 1980.

Kehrberg, Kent T. "Microcomputer Software Development: New Strategies for a New Technology."
AEDS Journal, vol. 13, Fall 1979, pp. 103-110.

_____. Learning Resources System at Elgin Com-
munity College (Application Brief GK20-1335-0
(6/80)). Data Processing Division, 1133 Westchester Avenue, White Plains, New York 10604.

Morlan, John, Classroom Learning Centers, Belmont,
California, Fearon, 1974.

Minnesota Educational Computing Consortium. A
Feasibility Study of Administrative Uses of
Microcomputers. 2520 Broadway Drive, St. Paul,
Minnesota 55113, May 1979.

Minnesota Educational Computing Consortium. A Guide
to Developing Instructional Software for the
Apple II Microcomputer. 2520 Broadway Drive,
St. Paul, Minnesota 55113, February 15, 1980.

Minnesota Educational Computing Consortium. Microcomputer Report of 1979-1980. (Report). 2520
Broadway Drive, St. Paul, Minnesota 55113, July
1979.

Moursound, D., ed. ES^3 Report. Eugene, Oregon:
Association for Computing Machinery, February
1980.

Moursound, David. "Some Thoughts on Reviewing Software." The Computing Teacher, vol. 7, June-July
1980, pp. 35, 37.

National Council of Teachers of Mathematics. An
Agenda for Action: Recommendations for School
Mathematics of the 1980s. Reston, Virginia: The
National Counsel of Teachers of Mathematics,
1980.

"New Software from MECC," Apple Education News
(periodic news source). Published by Apple Computer Inc., Issue 1, September 1979.

_____. On-Line Data Processing Systems for
Education Mean... (Brochure). Hewlett-Packard,
11000 Wolfe Road, Cupertino, California 95014.

Poirot, James L. and Groves, David N. Computer
Science for the Teacher. Sterling Swift Pub-
lishing, Manchaca, Texas, 1976.
_____. Computers and Mathematics. Sterling
Swift Publishing, Manchaca, Texas, 1979.
Radio Shack, Microcomputer Sourcebook for Educators,
pp. 12-16, Radio Shack, 1980.
Starbeck, April, Director of Publications. Star-
beck's Software Directory. Apple Computers.
11990 Doresett Road, Maryland Heights, Missouri
63043, 1980.
Taylor, Robert. The Scarsdale Project. Integrat-
ing Computing in the K-12 Curriculum. Report of
Teachers College, Columbia University. New
York, New York, 1980.
Texas Instruments, Inc. Texas Instruments Intro-
duces the TI-99/4 Home Computer. Printed in
U.S.A., 1979.
Tri-County Goal Development Projects. Course Goals
in Computer Education, K-12. Portland, Oregon:
Northwest Regional Educational Laboratory, 1979.
U.S. House of Representatives Committee on Govern-
ment Operations. Privacy Act of 1974. (Report
No. 93-1416). Washington, D.C.: U.S. Govern-
ment·Printing Office, 1974.
U.S. House of Representatives Committee on Science
and Technology Subcommittee on Domestic and
International Scientific Planning, Analysis and
Cooperation. Computers and the Learning Soci-
ety. (Report). Washington, D.C.: U.S. Govern-
ment Printing Office, 1978.
U.S. House of Representatives Committee on Science
and Technology and Committee on Education and
Labor Subcommittees on Science, Research and
Technology and Select Education. Information
Technology in Education: A Joint Hearing and
Workshop. Washington, D.C.: U.S. Government
Printing Office, 1980.

INDEX

ACM 17

Adjunct CAI 11

Administrative Func-
tions 2,31,33,44

Apple 6

Applications ... 1,21,25

Author CAI 11

BASIC 15

Batch System 4,5

BINGO 49

BUGS 54

Cable 3

CAI Advantages 12

CAI Authoring 11

CAI Disadvantages ... 12

CARDIAC 64,65

Class Attendance 34

COBOL 5

Complement Arithme-
tic 58

Computer Assisted In-
struction (CAI) ...
2,8,9,11,26,70

Computer Competen-
cies 17,19

Computer Data Proc-
essing 15

Computer Instruction. 14

Computer Literacy ...
15,17,70

Computer Mathematics. 14

Computer Systems 20

Computer Rationale .. 45

Display 29

Drill CAI 10

Electronic Blackboard. 3

FORTRAN 5

Funding 3

Games 47

Goals in Computer
Education 22

Grade Analysis 35

Grade Reporting 38

Graphics 13

Hands-Up 56

Hexapawn 59

IBM 27,38

Inventory 42

I HAVE (game) 51

Integrated Systems .. 70

Intelligent Terminal. 71

Interactive System .. 5

Laboratory Activi-
ties 81

Laboratory Centers .. 77

Laboratory Teacher .. 79

Mark I 1

Master File 32

Microcomputer 69

Microcomputer Labo-
ratory 72,74,75

Microcomputer Net-
work 70
Microcomputer Selec-
tion 80
Microprocessor 6
MOVIN' ON 47

National Science
Foundation 3
Non-Payroll Services. 42

On-Line System 5
Optical Scanning . 35, 37

Payroll 39
PET 27
Pilot System 11
Plato System 9, 11
Primary CAI 11
Programs 4

Radio Shack 27
Regional Service
Center 6
Room Utilization 40

Scheduling 38
Shifting 58
Simulation 10
Software Availabil-
ity 25
Software Guidelines . 27
Software Selection .. 27

Taxes 43
Terminal 5
Texas Instruments ... 27
Threats of Computers. 21
TRS-80 6
Tutor 9
Tutorial CAI 10